DEATH, DYING and DESSERT

Also by Susan A. Lieberman

- *Getting Old is a Full Time Job: Moving on from a Life of Working Hard*
- *The Mother-In-Law's Manual*
- *Venus in Blue Jeans: How Mothers and Daughters Can Talk About Sex*
- The REAL High School Handbook: How to Survive, Thrive and Prepare for What's Next
- *SUPER SUMMERS* (Editions for Houston, TX; Jacksonville, FL; El Paso TX; Springfield, IL)
- *NEW TRADITIONS: Redefining Celebrations for Today's Family* (Previously published as *Let's Celebrate*)
- *The KIDFUN Activity Book*

DEATH, DYING AND DESSERT
Reflections on Twenty Questions About Dying

Susan Abel Lieberman

For Michael, Jonathan, and Seth

Table of Contents

Introduction

How This Book Came To Be

It started with dessert, specifically with iced angel food cake. My husband and I both love the iced angel food cake from Moeller's Bakery in Houston. It seemed the perfect dessert for a dinner organized to discuss death and dying, so I drove across town to pick up a cake for our first gathering. When we had devil's food cake for our second dinner, Sally Dwyer said, "We should call this group Death, Dying and Dessert (DDD)." That was three years ago. We have been meeting since, usually every eight weeks or so, with a specific conversation topic for each gathering. The group has grown from six women to twenty-two. Usually, twelve to fifteen of us are able to participate on any given evening. Our ages range from almost fifty to just past eighty.

Our conversations about death and dying never feel morbid, but sometimes they are sad. One of us lost a daughter in a car accident. Five of us have been widowed. Most of us have seen our parents die as well as other family members. When one of the group talks about her own difficulties with loss or her fears, all of us have a wave of gratitude for sitting in a room with people speaking so intimately and honestly. But there is also lots of laughter.

We continue coming together because there is great pleasure in learning from each other's experiences and insights.

My friend Nancy Rust and I started the group as a subset of a larger professional women's organization to which we all belonged called The Transition Network, but a group could be neighbors, congregants, colleagues, extended family, and friends—whoever makes sense for the circumstances. You can find information in Appendix I on how to start a Death, Dying and Dessert group and a list of possible conversation topics. It certainly needn't be all women, and many in the group have wondered how to engage their partners in conversations like ours.

Nancy and I were motivated by our family situations, which brought home to us, quite painfully, how much we didn't know—and didn't know we didn't know—about aging, death, and dying. Nancy's father and my mother, within a few weeks of each other, landed in hospice care. But they didn't die. They didn't get worse. They got a bit better, and left hospice. They didn't get better enough to return to a full engagement with the world but were hanging on. My mother returned to hospice a year later during a bout of pneumonia. A year after that, at nearly ninety-six, she entered hospice for the last time and died twelve days later. Nancy's dad, whose cardiologist had predicted "six months at most," died five years from that first diagnosis, only the last few days clearly ill enough for hospice care again.

When our parents, who each had been driving, shopping, and living independent lives, first became ill and suddenly seemed to be approaching death, we were—well, we were stunned and a little crazy. It was scary and stressful and meeting at our favorite sushi place every couple of weeks to talk helped. What the talk kept returning to was how much we didn't know and how we could have made better decisions if we had had information and understanding sooner.

When my father died, I was in my early twenties. He had a heart attack crossing the street and was gone before he reached the curb. Then, I thought of death as an aberration. When my mother became ill, I was in my early sixties. Death now seemed more an intimation, a shadowy reminder that we all die. Gradually, it hit us that in the future, perhaps the near future, the concerns of death and dying would be focused on us, not our parents.

Because Nancy and I were so chastened by how ignorant we were of the issues that arise in aging and dying, we started talking about how to prevent others from falling into the same confusions and fears that we addressed. More sushi lunches led us to start the Y Collaborative with the mission of talking with healthy people about end-of-life issues. We chose the name because Y sits just before the end of the alphabet. If you look at it, it is a decision tree, and if you listen to it, it is a question.

This book is the outgrowth of all our Death, Dying, and Dessert discussions and of my work with the Y Collaborative, but it is deeply influenced as well by the work of so many other writers whose books have broadened my understanding of death and dying, who have informed, provoked, stimulated, and enriched me. I want this book to feel complete on its own, but throughout I give you the names of other books I have especially liked that elaborate on the questions at hand.

I am immensely grateful to the women who have participated in the Death, Dying, and Dessert conversations and who have taught me so much, both cognitively and emotionally. My warmest thanks to Marlys Barry, Lynn Bliss, Ann Butler, Cathi Collins, Pamela Daniels, Jaci Day, Sally Dwyer, Jo Fetterman, Anna Grassini, Dorothy Greenberg, Ginny Gremillion, Sue Jacobson, Liebe Ostrow, Barbara Rozek, Nancy Rust, Nancy Schwab, Claire Shumsky, Donna Siegel, Susan Stanton, Darlene Walker, Lue Gates Weiss, Sandy Wotiz, and Thelma Zirkelbach and to the people who have come to Y Collaborative talks and seminars and to the institutions that hired us.

I also want to thank, with great gratitude, the men and women who read and commented candidly on drafts: Andy Achenbaum, Lynn Bliss, Sue Cejka, Harvey Cummings, Andrea Eisenstein, Noll Evans, Mel Gallagher, Ginny Gremillion, Irene Heisinger, Susan Hoak, Nancy Rust, Marjorie Schultz, Carol Spong, Lou Gates Weiss, and Arline Worsham. Among them is a gerontologist, a therapist, an estate attorney, a geriatric care manager, a former director of human resources at a large urban hospital, a hospital ethicist, a healthcare recruiter, and a developmental psychologist—and a few readers whose gift is that they have no expertise with this material.

Special thanks to my husband, Dr. Michael Lieberman, who was my first reader and whose love, laughter, intelligence, and cups of tea sustain me in all things, and to my sons, who are understanding of my need to discuss this with them… frequently.

I am, of course, responsible for any errors, misphrasings, or misunderstandings, but my reviewers are responsible for helping me craft a better book and for encouraging me, which is so important when you are sitting alone, day after day, communing with only a computer. I feel lucky to have these people in my life.

1. Why Is Dying Important When We Are So Busy Living?

I t is clear that most of us understand that we will die. We just don't expect it to happen in our lifetimes.

When I'm at a social gathering and someone asks what I do for work, I tell them that I talk about death and dying with healthy people. The person who asks usually says something like "How interesting!" before turning the conversation elsewhere or, alternatively, turning himself elsewhere. Why discuss dying when we can talk sports, politics, fashion, food, travel… anything but death. I'm happy to gossip, brag about my kids and grandkids, or give my opinion about what's happening in the news. I try to keep my obsession with the value of discussing end-of-life issues in check. But here is what I want to say:

Look, denial is fine. It is normal to deny death. We are wired that way. But just, for a little bit, step outside of denial, get your paperwork in order, think about the options that face us, think about the fact that each of us will, in time, die. Talk with the people who are important to you. Get your hands around death and dying and then, if you wish, step right back into denial.

We will die. There is no escape. We may not be thinking about death, but death is thinking about us. The best of us die and the worst of us too. When we die is not dependent on our vices or virtues. Life, we so well know, is not fair, it just is. Belief in a higher power can give us a sense of calm and being cared for and it may help us manage our fears, but it cannot tell us what awaits us tomorrow. If, you might ask, if the end of life is inevitable, why give it a thought? Why not leave it in the hands of God or fate or chance?

Neither gods nor fate can write your will or sign your healthcare proxy. They cannot answer for your children the questions you did not want to answer about your decisions, your preferences, and your unspoken feelings. And, evidence suggests, the gods are not so good at reducing stress and chaos in the midst of a healthcare crisis. Perhaps their domain is in the hereafter, but we have to get past death and dying to understand that. The here and now demands some attention from us.

Listening to so many stories of difficulty and even disaster surrounding deaths of friends and family that could have been ameliorated with a little planning, I've turned into a missionary. The more I study and learn, the more I want to talk. I wish I could program this book onto everyone's car radio. You could listen for free, but it wouldn't stop playing until you completed the end-of-life paperwork, talked to your family, and given some thought to how you will make end-of-life decisions. Once you had done this, the radio program shuts off and you go right back to news, music, sports, and denial if you want.

Here are some reasons to think about death and dying while we are healthy:

1. Preparation invites better decisions.

Hanging on the edge of a precipice, engulfed in terror, is not the time or place to learn about emergency rock climbing procedures; you have to learn them before you start the expedition.[1]

I love this quote from Deborah Morris' wonderful book, *Talking About Death*. It is the first book I read about death and dying, and I continue to keep a copy on my bookcase. I must have given twenty copies as gifts. Morris writes in her introduction, "Changing the way we die requires that we change the way we look at death."[2] I hope this book contributes to that change.

When we fall into a life-threatening healthcare crisis, our brains go mushy. It is overwhelming, scary, often unbelievable. Our executive function, that part of the brain that helps us make rational decisions, commonly gets flooded, and we function with fight, flight, or freeze instincts. Eventually, we regain control, but by then, we may have made decisions that were not our best choices.

Or we can't make decisions because we have a tube down our throats or we are comatose. Families are much more likely to talk with us about dying and the choices we might make when it all seems hypothetical rather than when death is imminent.

It's so common, when given bad news, to ask, "Why me?" We feel picked on, cheated, angered. Of course, the simple answer to "Why me?" is "Why not you?" Since, sooner or later, it *is* going to be you, it can't hurt to learn about how to climb these rocks while calm rather than when you are hanging, as Morris writes, "engulfed in terror."

2. Laying Down Synaptic Pathways Helps Us Avoid Panic In A Crisis.

One reason I started our Death, Dying and Dessert conversations was a conviction that if we had time to consider difficult questions in advance, to work out what we believed and how we wanted to behave, it would help us in a crisis. We could create what I described to myself as synaptic pathways, tracks in our brain that would provide critical information and understanding when we needed it. But this was just supposition on my part or, I worried, maybe just wishful thinking.

Now, I have two reasons to think this hunch may be right. First, is the work of neuropsychiatrist and 2000 Nobel Prize winner Eric Kandel. Kandel won his Nobel for research on the physiological basis of memory storage in neurons. He found that short-term memory temporarily alters the connections in our brain, but that there is no anatomical change. It is long-term memory that creates "enduring changes that result from the growth of new synaptic connections." [3] In other words, Kandel finds that our brains are, indeed, helped by having time to embrace new beliefs that are there for us when we need them.

This belief in laying down synaptic pathways is also supported by my personal experiences. Our family knew we did not want our mother in the hospital. One visit there showed us how disorienting the hospital was for her and how it triggered functional losses that did not return. John Sloan's *A Bitter Pill. How the Medical System is Failing the Elderly* further convinced me that the frail elderly seldom fare well in hospitals that are better at treating symptoms and body parts than whole people. We decided that in the event of another serious difficulty, we would return to hospice care but not to a hospital. We had a Do Not Resuscitate (DNR) order posted on the refrigerator, and mom's caretakers had clear instructions not to call 911 but to call us and hospice. Still, one weekend when mom passed out from a vasovagal reaction from straining to move her bowels, the caretaker panicked and called 911 and then called us. We were ten minutes away. By the time we arrived, my mother was back to her usual self, and there were four large, good-looking, emergency medical technicians from the fire department in her living room. We need, they explained, to take your mother to the hospital.

"No," I said, "you can't do that. Really, it was a mistake to have called you. I understand that you are just doing your job, but we have a DNR order and we do not want her in the hospital."

"Ma'am," explained the spokesman, "you don't want to be responsible for killing your mother. We need to take her in."

Now, what do you say? Do I want to sign on to killing my mother? Is this a conversation I ever want to have? But, because I was so prepared not to admit mom to a hospital, I was able to hold my ground. Then they told me that a copy of a DNR was not acceptable. I needed the original. Not true, I knew, but what if I hadn't known that and crumpled.

Then they explained that I would have to talk by phone to their boss, the EMS medical director. He, too, asked me if I wanted to be responsible for my mother's death. It was those synaptic pathways that gave me the courage to say, "Yes."

Finally, these very nice men who were just doing their job left, and I looked at my hands. They were shaking uncontrollably. Without advance preparation, mom would have gone off in the ambulance. She didn't need to go. The best treatment for her was some love and attention, best administered at home.

It is unlikely we can imagine every possible scenario in advance or prepare for every option. But it is entirely likely that we can reach a point of view, a way of thinking about crises and their possible responses that will make coping in difficult moments easier.

3. Avoiding preparation can be expensive, financially and emotionally.

It can be expensive to ignore preparations for our inevitable act of dying. The cost may be in dollars or in family disharmony. Worst case, and estate attorneys tell us that the worst case is all too frequent, it is both.

We, if we are able to speak, can always override earlier decisions simply by saying so. The difficult moments are not when we decide to change our minds but when we are quite confused about what to do, when we can't think straight, when our families disagree, when our doctors have no guidance because we have refused to think about and plan ahead for end-of-life issues.

In later chapters you'll find detailed discussion about the paperwork that anyone over eighteen years old should have in place and how to complete it easily and, except for a will, at no cost. Appreciate that doing nothing is not really doing nothing. It is saying, "Okay government, you get to decide who gets my stuff and money. Okay, hospital people, you figure out how I want to die. Okay, family, if you disagree, stand outside my room and fight it out because I didn't want to think about it."

Facing finitude triggers the need for all kinds of decisions. For example, soon after you die, others will have to decide what to do with your body. Chapter 13 talks about funeral options, but for now, imagine your family gathered outside the room where you just died. They are sad and they are stressed, and they are trying to decide whether you should be cremated or buried.

If you have not expressed a preference, people will select their own, and they may not all agree. But let's imagine everyone knows the person who just died wanted a funeral that requires a casket. Where do you get that casket? Are you going online to shop and hope you like what arrives? Are you going to the funeral home where one of you believes the $6,000 number befits a beloved parent and another one of you thinks your parent would be horrified to put that kind of money into something buried in the ground? Now, you get to argue over who loved dad the most, who cares the most, who is cheap, who is greedy, who wants to show off. Really, you do *not* want to do this or anything like this, and you don't want the people who love you to find themselves in such a situation. Just help them out with a few directions that are ready and waiting when needed.

There is no reason to expect our family members will all see dying and death the same way. If we don't provide some direction, don't specify who is in charge, and don't make it known to all that it is *our* decision that this person is authorized to act on our behalf, we pave the way for family conflict. Such conflict is not necessary and not desirable.

4. It can take time to figure out what we want and to learn how to approach illness.

Our Death, Dying and Dessert group has been meeting now for about three years. It takes time to talk about all the subjects important to us and to let what we learn trickle into our brains. Remember, those synaptic pathways are formed over time, not in a moment. And the more we open ourselves to thinking about death, the more we find there is to learn.

Our conversations reduce our anxieties about aging and dying and help us figure out what we think will be right for us. It is so helpful to hear each other's opinions and stories. Your bad experience can save me from my own bad experience. Your emotional struggle can lead to my clarity. Your astounded expression at my pronouncement can make me reconsider what I'm thinking.

I used to joke that if I had an ingrown fingernail that hurt, I might tell the medical team it was time to stop all treatment. I was so worried about being kept alive too long that I put myself at risk for leaving too soon. Others of us were sure we wanted to stave off death no matter what but have come to feel that there are worse things than dying. Maybe we will find all this talk doesn't matter when directly facing our mortality in real time, but those of us who have faced the death of family members during the months we have been meeting report that our group has been hugely helpful.

A woman who joined the group a couple years ago says she had the paperwork completely organized for her mother-in-law, but the family never discussed end-of-life issues. Because of Death, Dying and Dessert conversations, she was the only one in the family to gather information about her mother-in-law's life, where she wanted to be buried, what funeral home to use, what type of service and where, what bequests she had beyond the will, and whether she still understood and agreed with her medical directives. "When she died last year unexpectedly, I knew what she wanted us to do and could help my husband who was unable to deal with any of the details." But, she continues:

> …the biggest bonus of our DDD group is that I began to think about my husband and me and our end-of-life issues. Previously, I had figured there was time for that later. Suddenly, I realized my husband, my sister, and I are the older generation. At first that was a truly frightening thought, particularly since our family did not discuss death or dying. But by thinking about the issues we will face, discussing them with others, getting ideas on how to handle them, thinking about what I want to do or not do (with the right to change my

mind, of course), laying some plans, and letting the family know about the plans, the end-of-life issues have become more familiar and less frightening. I find I spend less time dwelling on the end of life and more about what I have left that I want to do.

Another member of the group wrote:

My mother had just died a painful death from pulmonary fibrosis, and I had no desire to talk any more about dying, but several people in the DDD group mentioned that the conversations weren't a total downer, so I decided to see for myself.

I admit I haven't been good at following through with the paper projects I have assigned myself. Nonetheless, I have a much broader understanding of what I need to do. Deep down inside, I keep hoping that discussing sad topics such as handling life without a spouse, coping with incurable illness, etc. will better prepare me for when I am faced with these realities. I don't leave the DDD meetings particularly upbeat, but feel like I am helping myself better manage for future inevitable events.

Another woman reports feeling a surprising calm going up in the hospital elevator late at night when she knew her father was dying. "I remembered our conversations, and I felt I could cope."

Many of us find we feel less anxious about dying. Our oldest member is completing hospice volunteer training as her way of understanding what her own journey might be. Another just completed a memoir of the year her husband moved from the land of the well to the land of the ill. Perhaps Sally speaks for all of us when she says, "I crave dialogue with depth and, for me, Death, Dying and Dessert conversations are heartfelt in sincerity and touch a depth that is meaningful... And then there's dessert."

Here is another way all of us think we are benefitting from our conversations together. Many of us have struggled with parents who refuse to accommodate aging, then have an accident and make everyone's life more difficult. When our parents will not discuss what is going on with them and help us work out a sensible strategy, it makes us crazy. We get more shrill and more insistent, and they get more truculent. Not so good.

We see that the time for us to talk about when to stop driving, when to give up a big house, when to accept help with cleaning, bill paying, or shopping is not when the need is urgent. It's when the need doesn't yet exist. If we don't believe we will ever find ourselves in this space, when we arrive, we are shocked and resistant. Denial seems better than change. Until something bad happens.

So we have been talking about this among ourselves, wondering how we can prepare to be open to changes we might not like, how we can resist grumbling and demanding and making our kids' lives harder than necessary at no gain to ourselves. We talk about whether we have to hate the idea of moving in to senior living or even a nursing home, whether giving up the car keys is a terrible fate, how we can hear our children but also help them hear us. We talk about getting it into our brains that vulnerability, fear, and denial are normal but need to be addressed.

How much better if we can be the ones to initiate change, to suggest we give up driving, move to a different living arrangement, get some help with chores. Can we be so grown up that we tell our children this?

> When you begin to worry about my ability to manage, I grant you permission to come and talk, and I'll try my best to listen and respond rationally. If I can't, be patient, but don't let me put others at risk. I don't want you to insist on changes that are good for you but not for me, but I also don't want you to let me do harm to the family, so we need to work together.

Again, this is about laying down those synaptic pathways for long-term understanding. Conversations of loss are never easy or even welcome, but if we expect that one day we will need them and we think about how we might respond, the chances of having productive talk goes up. A couple of decades ago, I went to a weeklong workshop on Cape Cod, led by Daniel Levinson, who did groundbreaking research on the stages of adult development. Each day, a different panel of participants spoke about the challenges and opportunities for their stage. The last panel consisted of men and women older than sixty-five. One of them was a therapist in her eighties who spoke about the losses people in her stage of life endure. She told us the work of that stage was to compensate for the losses, to find ways to adapt to what was no longer the same for us. I remember few specifics of what was said that week, but I have not forgotten Ida Davidson and her compelling observations. Many of us are quite used to looking at alternatives, considering contingencies, and collecting data. We should not ignore those skills and refuse to acknowledge that there may well be decline and that there will certainly be death.

2. When Is It Time To Think About Dying?

All of us, of course, are dying. We start on that trajectory the moment we are born. We just hope our trajectory will be long and slow. Indeed, don't we really hope it will be like infinity… we approach it but never reach it? There are so many more immediate concerns. So many pleasures awaiting us, so many interesting adventures, so many urgent problems that need our attention right now. When, then, is it time to begin to grapple with the idea of death?

I know that most of you want to read "*later*." Mea culpa because the answer is "*right now*." We don't believe we are going to die tomorrow. Probably we are not. But one of us will. And, unless we are already ill, there is no warning light that goes off and says, "Next up."

The good news is that most of us, seventy-five percent, won't die until after age sixty-five. Three percent of Americans die before the age of fifteen. That always seems so wrong, so unfair, and completely impossible to prepare for. Then another twenty-two percent of us die between age fifteen and sixty-five. We talk about these deaths as aberrations that "shouldn't have happened." We don't expect them and often have trouble accepting them. As a consequence, most of us think we don't need to be prepared. We don't believe it will be us or those we love. How can we believe this? How can we hold that possibility? We know death happens in midlife to others, but we don't want to admit it could happen to us. It feels callous to insist it can and it may. Ah…but it can and may. And it is often these unanticipated deaths, for which no preparations have been made, that create serious chaos and distress.

For the seventy-five percent of us who will die after age sixty-five, death seems less aberrant if mostly unwelcome. We know there will be a final chapter, oh, maybe not the details but, for sure, death is on our agenda. Many people, maybe most people, prefer to imagine a soft landing, an ending in its most agreeable form. "If I get to choose, I will go to sleep and just not wake up," is a common sentiment. Or, "Whatever hits me, I want it to be fast and painless." Well, yes, me too. Statistically, however, we shouldn't count on it.

Twenty percent of us will experience some kind of organ failure—heart, lungs, and kidney among them. Twenty percent of us will be felled by cancer. Forty percent of us will die following an extended period of diminishment both in body and mind. The final twenty percent will die from one or another of less prevalent causes or disease trajectories. The older we are, the more likely death will not happen in an instant, but even if there is a slow unwinding, we remain reluctant to admit we are in the endgame.

For all of us dealing with terminal illness, the mindset we developed before we found ourselves in crisis can help us navigate the crisis. It is so much easier to talk honestly with family, fill out forms, and meet with lawyers while we are healthy. If we are dying and ill, our energies need to go towards caring for ourselves. If we are dying and not yet ill, we need to focus on what we most enjoy. As we'll discuss in the next chapter, the best antidote to dying is living.

It is not just those of us who are pushing through sixty and beyond who need to spend a little time considering what is important to us at the end of life. If you have just graduated from college, part of beginning your adult life should include putting paperwork in place. One woman in our group was in her office waiting to find out where to meet her daughter for lunch. That call never came because this lovely, lively, just starting-out-in-life young woman was hit by a car on the way to work and dead by the time she reached the hospital.

Everyone over eighteen ought to regard putting a first round of end-of-life paperwork in place as part of launching an adult life. If you are getting married, absolutely, you and your partner need to talk through your thoughts about death and dying and organize those darn forms. The manager of my branch bank told me of an organized young couple who came a week before their wedding to change the name of her account and set up a joint account that they didn't immediately fund. They didn't bother putting each other on their existing accounts or putting her name on his safe deposit box or completing a healthcare proxy. When he died in a boating accident during their honeymoon, she had no access to money in his account that she needed, nor could she get into the safe deposit box for important documents before a court was able to grant permission.

About to be a parent? Oh, for sure, you must have paperwork and conversations before the baby appears. I could make this more urgent with some stories, but they are just too painful for me to tell.

Are you traveling out of the country, especially in the third world? Prepare. Are you changing jobs, lifestyles, and partners? Prepare. Are your parents failing? Are you retiring? Prepare! In short, wherever you are in your adult life cycle, this is the time to start talking about how to be prepared for a healthcare crisis. You don't have to keep talking. Do it and be done until there is a change in your life that signals it is time to talk again.

3. Why Are We Afraid?

Andy Achenbaum, a gerontologist and historian at the University of Houston, shares my interest in the subject of death and dying and suggested I read Ernest Becker's Pulitzer Prize winning 1973 book *The Denial of Death*. I am a fast reader, but *The Denial of Death* took me three months to finish. Without sufficient background and so many ideas to explore, I would read a few dozen pages, ingest a couple of novels for a break, and return for more. I found the book brilliant and mind-altering.

Here is the core concept that so engaged me: "The irony of man's condition is that the deepest need is to be free of the anxiety of death and annihilation; but it is life itself which awakens it, and so we must shrink from being fully alive."[4] It is not the fear of dying that is the most-anxiety inducing but the fear of reality. Becker writes:

> The prison of one's character is painstakingly built to deny one thing and one thing alone: one's creatureliness. The creatureliness is the terror. Once admit that you are a defecating creature and you invite the primal ocean of

creature anxiety to flood over you. But it is more than creature anxiety, it is also man's anxiety, the anxiety that results from the human paradox that man is an animal who is conscious of his animal limitation. Anxiety is the result of the perception of the truth of one's condition.

Becker goes on to ask:

> What does it mean to be a *self-conscious animal?* The idea is ludicrous, if it is not monstrous. It means to know that one is food for worms. This is the terror; to have emerged from nothing, to have a name, consciousness of self, deep inner feelings, an excruciating inner yearning for life and self-expression—and with all this yet to die. It seems like a hoax, which is why one type of cultural man rebels openly against the idea of God. What kind of deity would create such complex and fancy worm food? Cynical deities, said the Greeks, who use man's torments for their own amusement."[5]

But Becker is not arguing for us to abandon faith. Rather, he believes that to face death opens the door to self-transcendence, to an understanding that our

> very creatureliness has some meaning to a Creator; that despite one's true insignificance, weakness, death, one's existence has meaning in some ultimate sense because it exists within an eternal and infinite scheme of things brought about and maintained by some kind of design by some creative force.[6]

Our desire to escape our anxiety about mortality inclines us to align ourselves with forces we believe are powerful, to see ways to connect with immortality. This is most conventionally a belief in God, but it can be an alignment with nature, with powerful people and ideas or with creativity.

The defeat of despair, for Becker, is not an intellectual problem but an invitation to live fully "in a partly self-forgetful way."[7]

I understand that to mean that we do need knowing to the degree that we can manage it, and then the best way to approach death is by finding pleasures—pleasure in working, creating, playing, loving—in as many places as we can and creating pleasures for others that light our way. Urging us to face death is an invitation to engage in life. Engagement with the world helps us feel part of the great cycle of being—which has a beginning, middle, and end—and we understand ending as part of the process.

We are all in the cycle of being, and it is normal to assume our most fruitful years are in the middle of that cycle, but there is evidence to suggest that the opportunity for selftranscendence can increase as we age. Research finds that people in their late eighties report being the most happy, while only a third of younger groups report being very happy.[8] Dr. Mark Agronin, a geriatric psychiatrist at the Miami Jewish Health Systems, within which sits the largest nursing home in Florida, works with elderly men and women living in this home, and he writes in *How We Age*:

In my work as a geriatric psychiatrist I have learned that *aging equals vitality, wisdom, creativity, spirit* and, ultimately, *hope.* For an increasing number of aged individuals these vital forces are growing day by day. (italics used by Dr. Agronin)[9]…Memory slows down but knowledge and wisdom increase.[10]

If we are afraid of dying because it is built into our biology to want self-preservation, if it is genetically predestined that we hanker to hang on, then we have to work at finding a way to accommodate both desire and destiny. We cannot alter biology, but we can reframe fears that the culture feeds to us and distinguish what is real and what is made up.

What doesn't kill us does not always make us stronger. Sometimes, it makes us weaker; sometimes it makes us crazy. What can help is to know what fears are realistic and which are based on incomplete or outdated information and prepare as best as is possible. We need to decide what we wish to endure and do so with accurate information.

There are real things to fear, not internal beliefs but external pressures. We need to name them, and we'll look at four fears that seem most potent. They are the result of external factors in our lives. We may find ourselves unable to manage these externalities, but if we can manage the internal response, we have a fighting chance of doing aging well.

1. We fear pain
The amazing gifts of medical technology allow us to treat diseases that not so many decades ago would have efficiently

finished us off. But the treatments are not without their own difficulties. Patients receiving chemotherapy talk of painful mouth sores, gastrointestinal systems that produce shifting agonies, aching bodies, endless fatigue, fever, diarrhea, or loss of appetite in the face of dangerous weight loss. It is not uncommon to believe the cure is worse than the illness. But many of us survive this awfulness and continue to live a satisfactory life. The challenge is to assess the odds and to consider stopping when the odds tell us we are playing a losing game.

For a time, the medical profession was more afraid of addiction than pain, and pain medications were doled out like calories in a weight loss program. Health professionals seem to be doing a better job of pain management now than in decades past, but pain is like food. It comes in many forms, calls up a variety of flavors, and requires different treatments for different pains and different people. A good compendium of kinds of pain and kinds of treatment can be found on the website of emedicinehealth (http://www.emedicinehealth.com/chronicpain/article_em.htm). Another good website is Caring Connections (www.caringinfo.org). See particularly the button at the top of the home page entitled "Live Without Pain."

If we think about the ways we might manage pain in advance, we can be more prepared to ask questions that will yield real data. We need to help our doctors talk with us candidly and without fear. (See Chapter 17.)

Pain management is too complicated to address here, but there is some useful advice that comes from pain experts:

A. Don't ignore pain. Try to describe the intensity and duration of the pain. One helpful way to understand pain is to keep a pain diary. Describe what seems to trigger the pain and when it is lessened. If pain persists for too long, it sets up brain pathways that make the pain more persistent and difficult to treat. The body starts looking for it.

B. If you are in the hospital and have continued pain, don't hesitate to ask for a palliative care consult. Palliative care is a subspecialty that is spreading rapidly in our hospitals. Its focus is on pain reduction and is available, unlike hospice, to people who are not presumed to be dying in six months and who may want to continue aggressive treatment while managing pain.

C. Know that mental stress can provoke physical pain. Don't be embarrassed to use the mental health professionals who are expert at dealing with emotional pain. It is not a weakness to need this kind of help any more than it is a weakness to have your arm set if it is broken. It is a strength to be wise enough to discern a need and find help early on.

2. We fear dependency

Could it be that the worst thing about dependency is that we don't think it should happen to us? It is virtuous, we know, to be strong, self-reliant, and autonomous. That makes it difficult when we need help. What if we expected that in the cycle of development there might come a time when, as when we were young, we had to rely on others to help us? If we saw it as natural would it be quite so bad?

We may have repaired companies or cars, written books or painted houses, raised successful families or managed all by ourselves—whatever we have done, we have done in our own way. And now, perhaps, we will find ourselves needing others for such basic functions as feeding, toileting, and moving. We may think that there is no dignity in needing this kind of help, but is it true? Is there a way to accept help, even if it has distasteful characteristics, with dignity?

I have told my children that there may be a day when I need their help, and while I don't expect them to give up their lives to service mine, I do expect them to do what they can. But I have a role too, and it is not to resist, not to be so stubborn that I refuse to have a reasonable conversation. It is not to reject help and find I cause myself harm. It is not to be so grumpy that everyone is miserable. I remember telling my sons that they didn't have to like memorizing the multiplication tables, they just had to do it. I might not like what life deals, but one form of control is deciding how to adapt to our circumstances with grace. Another is deciding when to keep fighting death and when to yield.

3. We fear dementia

We fear any kind of disease. We worry about cancer and stroke and other disabling or life-ending illnesses. But Alzheimer's disease and other forms of dementia seem to be a fear that reaches beyond the normal fear of illness. We do not want our brains stolen from us while the rest of us stays strong. We do not want to forget whom we love and where we are going. We do not want to give up being ourselves since it took us so much effort and care to become that self.

Alzheimer's disease causes many losses. For one friend, however, his father's dementia brought a gain:

> My father was pretty rough. He was bipolar and people, most especially his family, found him difficult. About five years ago, he slipped into serious dementia. It is as if it removed a cloud from his inner self and allowed his sweetness to come out. He doesn't know I'm his son but only that I'm someone familiar. He is cheerful with me and with his caretakers. I have come to have fonder feelings for my father these last years than I had before, and I'm grateful for that.

My stepfather, Sam, had Alzheimer's. The disease probably began long before my mother recognized something was wrong. Sam started drinking more than usual and, in retrospect, we imagine he was trying to self-medicate his fears. Mom was determined to take care of Sam at home, even though he liked to wander away and get lost or fire the sitters she hired to help her out. Finally, we, her children, surrounded her and insisted she consider using a care facility. "Mom, at this rate, you are going to die before Sam. We are losing you. You never smile any more. You are losing weight. And you are not saving Sam."

Sam spent several years in a nursing home. Finally, he had a stroke and, in spite of a DNR order, the nursing home called 911, and he went off to the hospital. When he returned to the nursing home, his hands were strapped down so he would not pull out his feeding tubes. The nursing home administrators refused my mother's requests that they stop all treatment and untie him. "How," they asked her, "can you let this sweet man die?" My mother had begun legal proceedings against the nursing home when Sam, blessedly, died on his own. Circumstances have much improved since Sam died over twenty-five years ago, but the difficulties of the disease remain.

There is an increasing amount of information about how to manage Alzheimer's and other forms of dementia. The very experienced social worker at the Houston and Southeast Texas chapter of the Alzheimer's Association recommends two books that both caretakers and people newly diagnosed with Alzheimer's report finding helpful: *Alzheimer's Early Stages* by Daniel Kuhn and *Living Your Best with Alzheimer's* by Lisa Snyder. There is, for the moment, no cure for Alzheimer's, but we have learned a great deal since my mother struggled to cope.

One difficult matter to consider before there is any sign of mental loss is whether we wish our lives to be extended by warding off illnesses like pneumonia or inserting feeding tubes as was done with Sam. Sometimes, as Alzheimer's or other brain disorders progress, we lose the ability to feed ourselves and, often, an interest in food. Many nursing homes insist on having feeders, people who feed patients. It is common in these circumstances, eventually, to insert a feeding tube. If we do not eat or drink, we die. How do we want our family to manage feeding? An advocate for allowing us to die by withholding hydration and nutrition is Stanley A. Terman, Ph.D., M.D. You can read his lengthy discussion of this in *The Best Way to Say Goodbye--A Legal, Peaceful Choice at the End of Life.*

4. We fear poverty

We have worked for decades. We have provided, coped, found ways to meet our needs. What if we can no longer do it? What if we run out of money, and we are unable to make any more. What if our families cannot or will not take us in and we are deposited somewhere to be leftovers? What if they run to our aid, and we are the cause of financial hardship for people we love so much? Again, the time to consider this is not when the dike is breaking. There are strategies that families can use to make it easier to qualify for Medicaid assistance, but they should be put in place at least five years before Medicaid may be required since certain actions taken in those sixty months before applying for help may make us ineligible for the help.

If we think we might need Medicaid, we may not have many resources now, so it may sound odd to recommend spending money to figure out how to qualify, but if possible, it's a good idea to consider the services of an eldercare lawyer who understands Medicaid. A decade back, the six children of Asian immigrants lost their father. Their mother wanted sell her house, sign over her modest assets to her children, and "live simply." One of the children had the foresight to hire an eldercare lawyer who helped the family create a trust that would allow their mother, in time, to receive assistance if necessary. The trust would also protect some assets in the event that the children wished to provide additional care that they could not afford privately and the state would not offer. It also protected these siblings from arguing in the future. It was, according to the family member who paid the bill, "worth much more than we paid."

Two places to look for resources and tips are:

- http://elderlawanswers.com/elder_info/medicaid-rules.asp (Medicaid rules)
- http://www.eldercarelink.com/Legal-and-Financial/Medicaid-Spend-Down-and-Personal-Assets-Tips-for-Eligibility.htm

To be afraid is not foolish. The danger is to allow ourselves to diminish our lives worrying about possible events over which we have no control, but it is entirely rationale to use worry to spur us to try to prevent difficulties. When our situation feels grim, it can be deeply annoying to have others pretend the sun will be out any minute. Susan Jacoby, in her painfully honest book *Never Say Die: The Myth and Marketing of the New Old Age,* says:

> Laying claim to the right to feel rotten about what is happening can free up energy for the fight to live as well as possible through whatever life hands out as we grow older…Hope is not incompatible with realism, but it is incompatible with the expectation that things are going to turn out well if we only conduct ourselves well. Inflated expectations about successful aging, if the body imposes a cruel old age, can lead to real despair.[11]

When we believe that if we exercise, eat right, keep busy, and have that most American of virtues, a positive mental attitude, then we can escape any difficulties, we are at risk to find we have just kicked ourselves from behind. The more we deny the possibility of difficulty, the more we are likely to be undone if difficulty descends. We want to hope we can keep whatever difficulties come our way from determining all aspects of our life. A friend dates a man who is in his mid-sixties. Until a few years ago, he was a competitive tennis player, a hiker and biker who liked to move quickly through the world. A case of spinal stenosis has made even walking difficult. He can barely get himself from his car to our front door with the help of two canes. He can't fight the stenosis, but he is working hard not to let it define who he is but to be only one characteristic of a complex self.

Consider Agronin again: "The commandment to 'rise up before the aged' (*Leviticus* 19:32) is not just a call for the young to respect their elders, but for the elders themselves 'to rise up before age' and continue to pursue their enhanced ability for spiritual fulfillment."[12] And what is our "spiritual fulfillment?" It is anything that gives our life meaning. It can be forgiveness, gratitude, loving-kindness. It can be reveling in the pleasures of a new baby, in flirting with a ninety-year-old; it can be remembering life's pleasures with joy or winning at the bridge table. For our friend with the canes, it is launching a new and satisfying romance. Or it can be refusing to be a kindly, benign old person who smiles when referred to as "honey."

In reading and talking, I have become convinced that some of what we dread is not because it is dreadful but because we have been acculturated to believe it is dreadful. If we focus only on what we have lost, on the difficulties we now endure and the limitations to our physical world, we are going to have a harder struggle. Vitality in old age is a mind game. As with most games, the earlier we start to consider how to play it well, the better we are likely to be.

For example, many of us dread living in a facility for seniors. A college friend's sister, in her eighties, jumped from an upper story balcony to her death from a conviction that moving to an assisted living facility would make her unrelievedly miserable. She might have given it a try first if she had talked with our eighty-two-year-old cousin whose physical condition forced her to move into assisted living, only to find that the increased sense of safety, ready socialization, and good care made her happy. No, she would not tell you it was better than being fifty and living in a lovely home with a car in the drive and money in the bank. But it was better than the chapter just before it and nowhere near as bad as she imagined.

It is not honest to say there is nothing to fear. Susan Jacoby writes:

> Dwelling on the inevitable losses of old age is considered a form of depression, to be treated in every case rather than respected, in some instances as a realistic response to irremediable trouble, pain, and loss. I believe that an honest look at the prevalence of bad, worse, and worstcase scenarios is a precondition—*the* precondition—for figuring out how to improve these scenarios.[13]

Years ago, I heard a speaker explain fear as "false expectations already realized." So here's the tension: On the one hand, we do not want to waste old age on being fearful and fretting about events that may never happen. On the other hand, being realistic about the future and preparing for it allows us to manage difficulty better. There is a difference between being realistic and prepared and being afraid. Preparing for the inevitability of death is not the same as dying, just as imagining a meal is not the same as eating it. I don't believe that preparation can alleviate all problems nor do I think I will be able to adapt to any circumstance, but I do believe that I can handle aging and decline better if I do not pretend it is impossible for me.

4. What Does Death Look Like?

At an early Death, Dying and Dessert meeting, we decided we would each bring a picture representing what death looks like. What image might you have brought?

Here are the pictures I remember:

1. A traditional skeleton dressed in a hooded cloak.
2. An angel that seemed to come from a Renaissance painting.
3. A child's rainbow sheltering flowers, trees, and sun.
4. An early woodcut with a skull and crossbones.
5. A blank sheet of paper.

Perhaps, we should have added a picture of a little boy popping out from behind a rock and saying BOO!! Doesn't death look surprising?

It matters how we imagine death. Our stories influence our behavior. If death is that hooded, grimacing skeleton, we are likely to feel frightened. The more we fear death, the more we risk anxiety, even in good health, and emotional suffering as we approach the end-of-life. If it's true that misery loves company, it may help to remember that everyone we know...and don't know...is also going to experience death.

I have an odd mantra: *Something unwelcome will happen.* I know that some will consider this depressing, ignoring that positive mental attitude so many self-help books urge on us. I don't see it that way. It isn't pessimistic or optimistic, it just is. I don't know if that unwelcome event will be fast or slow, sooner or later, but I do know it will come. When it comes, I don't want to ask, "Why me?" I want to be prepared to ask, "What now?" And knowing something difficult will happen in the future serves to make me all the more committed to grab life by the hands right now. Seeing the reality of death coming one day but not fearing it can heighten the intensity of life.

In his wise and honest award-winning book, *How We Die,* Dr. Sherwin Nuland describes, chapter by chapter, the major causes of death. (See box at the end of this chapter.) It's an excellent book for those who want a more specific understanding of what death may look like.

"I just can't fathom that one day I won't be here," my eighty-year-old friend proclaims. I, a woman of great imagined control, feel astounded by knowing that when I depart, the world will keep on managing just fine without me. But depart we will. And the world will go on. And what is there to say but, perhaps, "Thank you world for your gifts now." I know this world is chaotic, full of venality, aggression and irrationality. But I like those sun, moon, and stars, those spring seasons, the inventions and diversions, curiosities, opportunities, and possibilities. I would like to get as close to being all used up as I can.

I fantasize saying to death with a wave of my jeweled hand, "Oh whatever. Just take my body but leave ME. I'm not done here." How annoying that our souls, our minds, our spirits, that essence of our humanity are housed in time-limited bodies. Our greatness is tethered to the ground, literally, by our skeletal system, and when repairs can't keep it patched together, we see our bodies crumble. How ridiculous that we are going to vanish from this earth, at least in our current physical form, just because a heart stops beating. Or would it be more ridiculous if we just kept stockpiling our ancestors and no one left this world?

We all know there is no bargaining. Do you know the story of Samarra?

A merchant in Baghdad sends his servant to the marketplace for provisions. Shortly, the servant comes home white and trembling and tells him that in the marketplace he was jostled by a woman, whom he recognized as Death, and she made a threatening gesture. Borrowing the merchant's horse, he flees at top speed to Samarra, a distance of about 75 seventy-five miles, where he believes Death will not find him. The merchant then goes to the marketplace and finds Death, and asks why she made the threatening gesture. She replies, "That was not a threatening gesture, it was only a start of surprise. I was astonished to see him in Baghdad, for I had an appointment with him tonight in Samarra."[14]

What follows our appointment with death is all interpretation. Do some of us burn in eternal hell? I can't imagine a higher power that takes such a punitive approach to eternity. But what I believe should bear no relevance to what you believe. We may think about what is next in whatever way gives us comfort and meaning. I want to celebrate every faith, any belief, when I say it doesn't matter what we choose. I understand that some of us are sure our beliefs are the right ones and others of us will certainly regret not realizing this. But absent any data, I am going to go with the notion that whatever gives you comfort, assuming it is not harming others, is just fine.

Talk to any gods you wish. Cast a spell on any devils. Pray in whatever ways bring hope and sustenance. Or don't, as you wish. Dance and sing or bow and bend in celebration of anything. Having rituals, celebrations, familiar acts that ground us in our culture and our community are helpful in keeping darkness at a distance. Religion does that for many. So does nature or satisfying work or family. Damn, go for it all. It's hard work making a good life, especially in light of its scary finitude. Whatever helps defang the fears is usually a good idea. Just remember that death looks like whatever picture you bring to the party.

Number of Deaths for the Leading Causes of Death in the United States, 2011

- Heart disease: 599,413
- Cancer: 567,628
- Chronic lower respiratory diseases: 137,353
- Stroke (cerebrovascular diseases): 128,842
- Accidents (unintentional injuries): 118,021
- Alzheimer's disease: 79,003
- Diabetes: 68,705
- Influenza and pneumonia: 53,692
- Nephritis, nephrotic syndrome, and nephrosis: 48,935
- Intentional self-harm (suicide): 36,909
- All causes: 2,437,163

Source: http://www.cdc.gov/nchs/fastats/deaths.htm

5. What Is Old?

I turned seventy this summer, and I know I should be pleased when I am told, "My heavens, you don't look seventy!" Of course a bit of me IS pleased. But I usually respond, "But this is what seventy looks like." In fact, what does seventy look like? What if I looked my age and not younger? If someone said, "Ah, yes, that is the age I would have guessed for you," should I be offended or upset? Are we so put off by aging that our first impulse is to reassure someone that, in fact, they have, improbably, escaped?

No one is eager to look old and wrinkled, but if we are aging, it is normal that we begin to look older. Seventy may be the new fifty, but how many seventy-year-olds would pass for fifty? I am not one of them. I don't look fifty. I don't feel fifty, and I don't think in the same ways I did when I was fifty. I have done fifty. Now it is my time to do seventy, and I am hoping I can do it with grace, with comfort about where my long and rich years have brought me.

If we are not getting old, we are dead. There is no elixir. Of course, there are lots of things we can…and *should*… do to maintain ourselves as well as we can. One of the best is my least favorite.[15] Exercise helps just about everybody, and I love to avoid it. My trainer keeps asking, "Don't you feel better after we work out?" I think he feels better than I. I feel tired and, usually, hot. I show up for thirty minutes three times a week because I know I need to. I feel like the dog, and I think of Chad, my trainer, as the dog walker. Without the walker, I would be a house dog for sure. I am happy writing at my computer, reading in my big chair, managing various business requirements on the phone, sitting down. I do a three-mile loop in the park two mornings a week with a friend. It is the pleasure of our talking that gets me there, not the walking. I do it because I know it is good for me, because I want to be able to play with my grandchildren and take walks with my children.

Why am I so convinced that this little bit of exercise… and what I do is barely adequate…is so important? It is according to people like Sherwin Nuland. Nuland, a physician who teaches surgery and the history of medicine at Yale University, has written several books including *How We Die: Reflections on Life's Final Chapter,* which won the 1994 National Book Award, and the graceful, informative *The Art of Aging: A Doctor's Prescription for Well-Being.* Reading these thoughtful, informative, and hopeful books makes the need for exercise so clear.

Nuland believes it isn't so much death we want to delay as it is our gradual deterioration. The goal, he explains, ought not to be to live longer but to live well for a longer part of the time we have on this earth. We want to spend as little time as possible moving from healthy to frail, where we are more and more vulnerable to disease that leads to death.

Nuland writes:

> Though all of the body's systems lose elements of function as the years pass by, it is in the muscles and the bones that major problems are likely to be most frequent, and these problems are almost as obvious as such developments are in an organ as visible as the skin. Among the most obvious changes is the decrease in muscle and the increase in fat. Musculoskeletal inadequacy is the single most common cause of debility in the old.[16]

If we think that because we are aging and things feel more difficult, we can give up making efforts to stay limber and active, we are likely to grow weaker still. And then we increase our chances of dying sooner rather than later.

But if you have been a slouch, take heart. "It is consistently shown that strength can be almost doubled within six or eight weeks in the oldest old, merely by a supervised regimen of high-intensity resistance training and weights." [17] Muscle strength, so important to ward off frailty, can be preserved and regained by exercise. This is why I show up at the gym and walk and, when my husband can cajole me, swim laps. It is so aberrant that many people are more afraid of talking about death than they are afraid of not exercising. It is so much easier to buy new makeup, be fitted for a toupee, or get a Botox treatment to look better than to do the exercises that will actually make us better.

I don't know how to fight the stigma of aging that is pervasive in the culture. Perhaps, the best I can do is to work on fighting it in myself and my family. For myself, I think about how to balance competing realities. One reality is the "I don't look seventy" one. I imagine myself a cute thing and push away negative thoughts that may subtly encourage me to give in to slowing down. But the other reality is that I am getting older, and I do sometimes need to slow down and to think more carefully about how to use my physical and emotional resources. How can I deny aging and accept aging simultaneously?

I have been mulling over this conundrum for months. I realized our thirty-nine-year-old son had, unconsciously I think, also been puzzling the same question. It kept appearing in the guise of not so funny jokes. When I finally got my own puzzlement in perspective, I began to understand his and found myself writing this letter:

Dearest Seth,

Seth, because I am so interested in death, dying, and aging, I am especially aware of the fact that you frequently joke about our aging. I know you mean it in a lighthearted way. I also think the jokes come from a more fearful place, that place in all of us that does not want to see our parents age, decline, and die.

Your jokes have helped me to think about what I want to write about aging, and I want to try that out on you as I go.

On the one hand, I know I am getting older and that it brings some limits. I don't have as much energy or ambition as I did in earlier decades. I cannot walk as long as I used to without feeling tired. I cannot lift as much or stay up as late. I don't want to pretend that I am not aging because if I were not getting older, I would be dead.

That said, there is a careful balance between being aware of the aging process and the need to pay closer attention to one's body and to reasonable limits and to the importance of not paying so much attention that I begin to think of myself as old and let that stand as an excuse for giving in or giving up or sitting down.

What adult doesn't hate the thought of losing independence, of facing decline and loss? Much as we hate it, I think our children also hate it for different reasons. We don't want our parents to die. We want our parents to keep being our parents, not our adult children. We want to know that they can take care of us long after we stop wanting them to. And while we are willing to take care of them, really who wants to do that? All of this makes aging a fearful thing. And that fear seems to make our conversations about aging stifled and awkward. We use the language of sports: you can do it; come on now, push on; I'm rooting for you; I know you will win. We joke. We deny. We lie. We pretend.

I saw with Nana and with the parents of many friends that the unwillingness to address decline, the insistence of not making any changes and not admitting the need for help can, in fact, make aging more dangerous and difficult. An extreme example is the refusal to give up driving.

When a little help would go a long way, we parents resist because we fear we open the door to having our children take control. They don't know how to talk with us, and we are no better. We don't really know how to talk with them about this thing that scares us.

At seventy-one and seventy, Dad and I don't feel OLD but we don't feel young. We expect to have a good decade or more and to be able to enjoy so much of what now brings us satisfaction. We don't want you to see us as fifty, and we don't mind honest discussions about what the future is bringing. For example, your concern about estate options is a good example of sensible talk. But the jokes…they cut too close to the bone to be funny. Joking about our being old makes us feel old and that actually runs the risk of making us older.

So, how does a loving, sensible son like you manage his fears and ours and give voice to what you see and what may concern you without playing into stereotypes or being demeaning, which I know you would never intentionally do?

Maybe you can help me figure out the answer so I can write about it. I know it has something to do with speaking from the heart, with naming fears and hopes…but I'm still groping. What do you think?

Love,
Your seventy-year-old mother

After I wrote this letter on my computer, I e-mailed it to my son asking him what he thought about including it in this book and, more importantly, what he thought about my take on this. Here is what he e-mailed back:

Mom-

Thank you so much for sharing. I think you have touched on some really important and deep topics, but I think you read too much into the jokes. They really are throwaway comments that are obviously noise and not signal. They fill the air, and I'll stop. I don't even realize I am making them half the time, or that I make that many--but I do see that they are registering with you negatively. I apologize, it was not my intent, and so let me correct this action. It's easy to do. Poof, gone.

That said I think you are very much right about the other items in your note. I do fear death, but I also know it will be very hard on me to watch you and dad age, though without question, easier than it would have been say ten to twenty years ago. I think for me the reason is that you two have always been a source of strength for me, and while I am lucky that nothing really bad has ever happened to me (and hopefully won't) when thing go sideways, I have always known I could rely on you two emotionally, financially and physically. Knowing I always have had such a strong safety net has helped push me to be who I am today.

And so while Julie (and to some degree Jonathan) serve as a pillar of strength for me—as it should be it—I recognize the gradual shift from me depending on you to you depending on me. That saddens me a little, and I think might scare me a bit too. But it also gives me hope and joy. You two have done so, so much for me. I can only pass it on to my kids the same way and then support you in your time of need as you did me. For you to be able to rely on me when you are in need of it will be a very rewarding for me personally. I know no one wants that situation, but know that I will always be there for you and dad no matter how sick or crazy you get. And know that I understand and respect your wishes of who you are, how you have lived your life, and what your values are and will be true to them for you even if you cannot be for yourself. Always.

We can talk more when I get back from Kansas City— on my way now. But I will stop with the dumb age jokes. Can you end one comment for me? You keep saying "My sons love their father unconditionally but love me in a different more complicated way." It's not true, you have it wrong. I love you unconditionally in a way that is just as deep and primal as dad. Really. Truly. And now I am tearing up.

You loving son forever,
Seth

I teared up too.

6. Can We Afford to Die?

As I was writing this chapter, I found four lines from Kingsley Amis in Christopher Hitchens small but powerful book, *Mortality*:

> Death has this much to be said for it;
> You don't have to get out of bed for it.
> Wherever you happen to be
> They bring it to you—free.[18]

You don't have to pay to stop breathing. But don't get confused. Keeping someone from ceasing to breathe is not free. And figuring out how to breathe more easily is not free. If dying can be done at no cost, avoiding dying is likely to be expensive.

It is not even interesting to write that healthcare is costly. If you don't know this, you may, in fact, have already stopped breathing. Ah, but you say you are sufficiently old that you have Medicare and supplemental health insurance or you have employee health coverage, so you needn't worry. Maybe. Maybe not. Medicare is great. It covers lots of interventions. But it doesn't cover everything. *CNN Money* reported that "a recent Mount Sinai School of Medicine study that found that the out-of-pocket expenses for Medicare recipients, in the last five years before their death averaged about $39,000 for individuals, $51,000 for couples and up to $66,000 for people with long-term illnesses like Alzheimer's."[19] Medicaid, which is for those of us who just run out of money, is also great. It covers nursing home care for those who don't have the funds to pay. But it also doesn't cover everything and it has complicated rules. The rules for both programs favor providing financial support to cover acute care. Chronic care, those problems that must be managed over time, usually out of the hospital, can bring uninsured costs.

"And you will know the truth and the truth will set you free." Although these words are usually used in a biblical context, I am using them here to refer to a grasp of insurance law. Not as uplifting, perhaps, but also revelatory. This should be paired with another familiar quote: "What you don't know can't hurt you." In fact, what you don't know can kill you. My husband was chair of pathology at a major medical school and hospital. I have a Ph.D. in public policy. After he retired, we ended up with no health insurance for about eighteen months, only the last six of which did I understand we were uninsured. How this happened is a long story, but it gave painful relevance to the second quote. And it can happen to you, I'm sure.

So, what can you do?

First, long before you retire, you need to develop a financial plan with different contingencies. You need to decide if it makes sense to buy insurance for personal care that covers nursing home and home care. Many of us get obsessed with saving money to send children to college and forget we might need money to send us to somewhere.

Second, you need to read that government book, *Medicare and You* (http://www.medicare.gov/), which explains in mostly clear language what Medicare does and doesn't provide. Yes, any number of things is more fun to read. Plow through it anyway and get some grasp of this.

Another helpful book is Maria Loughlin Carley's *Health Insurance. Navigating Traps and Gaps*, which alerts us to all the complications of health insurance. With The Affordable Health Care Act, also known as "Obamacare," moving into place, coverage should become easier, but we have to understand the rules and regulations, even if we would rather not, and many us would really rather not. All coverage has limits, and it is helpful to know when we might reach them. I think a group in your place of worship or neighborhood discussion group with everyone sharing in the reading and explaining is, perhaps, the easiest way to get a grip. If the group has enough members, experts may be willing to come and make short presentations.

Attempting a summary of all the rules may only delude you into thinking you understand all this. Instead, I want to offer three nuggets of advice meant to save you money and craziness.

1. Slow down

Sometimes, we don't have the option of time. In the case of stroke victims, administering the drug tPA within three hours of the onset of symptoms is critical. If more time elapses, the drug is much less effective in preventing brain change.

Unless we must administer a drug quickly, stop serious bleeding, put body parts back in the body or other emergency maneuvers, the most important thing we can do when an unexpected crisis appears is B…R…E…A…T…H…E…

Take a few deep breaths. Then take a few more. Try a mantra, maybe something like, "It is what it is and we will do what we can," or "This too shall pass," or "God grant me the serenity to accept the things I cannot change; courage to change the things I can; and wisdom to know the difference." Repeat as needed.

A scare triggers our fight, flight, or freeze reflex. Our executive function, that rational front part of our brain, shuts down or slows and is frozen, or we leap into action impelled by a more primitive part of the brain. Often we do have the time to think before we act, if only for a few hours, a day, or (better yet) several days while we research, reflect, and recalibrate.

For example, my business partner's dad was in the hospital for blood clots. She came in one day and was told his doctors had scheduled him for surgery the next day to insert a mesh screen to prevent clots from traveling to his heart and killing him. With deer-in-the-headlights surprise, she said, "Okay." A few hours later, she started asking herself questions. Her dad had been in hospice care until recently. No one in the family, including the patient, was focused on a longer life. Why should her father have to go through this surgery and risk infection, she wondered. She called the hospital and told them to cancel the procedure until she and her father better understood what was planned for him. With a fuller explanation, both agreed that he should go home, not to the surgical suite.

2. Don't procrastinate

Don't wait until you or your family members fall into a healthcare crisis. The whole point of this book is to motivate you to prepare for dying while enjoying life. The time to talk with family members about death is while you are healthy. Work your way through all twenty questions that headline the chapters of this book, make notes in the margins or on the flyleaf or on your refrigerator notepad. Decide what you want to do and then decide when and how you will do it. Be assured that anything you decide can be revised or revoked.

Procrastination is normal. Do not, repeat, *do not*, fall into this trap. Make a commitment to someone important in your life about completing the necessary paperwork and having at least one conversation with family. Tell this person by what date you will do this, and ask that he or she please help you be accountable to yourself.

Maybe it takes an appointment with an estate attorney to get you started. Maybe it requires a family email in which everyone agrees to a date. Maybe you need to book out an evening or a weekend afternoon, go www.ycollaborative. com and fill in the forms on line, print them, and have them witnessed that afternoon. Do it with a friend or spouse. Do not let life catch you out and make you regret you did not attend to this.

3. Buy expert advice

Recently, I heard Jane Gross speak. Gross worked as an award-winning journalist for the *New York Times*. Her brother is also a journalist. They believed in their ability to frame questions, uncover data, identify resources, and arrive at good answers. When their mother became unexpectedly ill, they believed they could solve her problems themselves. Gross' speech and her excellent book, *A Bittersweet Season*, made it clear that they did not know what they didn't know and made mistakes that they regretted.

Gross noted in her talk that she frequently advises friends to hire a geriatric care manager and, almost always, they ignore the advice, thinking they can figure things out on their own. So, hire a geriatric care manager or hire an eldercare lawyer or, depending on your circumstances, hire both. My estate attorney is one of three sisters. Her parents lived in a different state and there was lots of fussing about what to do and who would do it. Finally hiring a care manager helped them make better, faster decisions and assign responsibilities. I hired a care manager when my husband and I were leaving town for extended periods, and I wanted mom's caretakers to have a local resource in case they needed help. Friends with parents in other states have used care managers to check in on their parents and make sure they found the resources they needed to continue to live independently.

In our Death, Dying and Dessert group, several women have never married. They don't have partners, children, and, in some cases, siblings to be there to support them. We have decided one good strategy for people who feel they lack a support system is to develop a relationship with a geriatric care manager, younger than they, in advance of need.

What do geriatric managers do? In short, they advise you on what to consider and how to weigh your decisions. They help you identify needed resources. In some instances, they can act on your behalf and provide services. (See Appendix II for a more complete discussion of geriatric care managers.)

A good time to connect with a case manager is at the first sign of healthcare difficulties that may require difficult decision-making. Jane Gross talks about her family's very quick decision to move their mother from Florida back to New York and the need to find a new senior living facility. In two weeks, they had signed a contract for a new residence, moved their mother, and emptied her old apartment. It was only after this was done that they realized they had put their mother in a living arrangement that did not permit the use of private aides, and they needed one.

Telling you to buy advice, breathe, and give up procrastination does not immediately put more money in your bank account, but these recommendations can save you money and stress. Regardless of our bank account, we die. Regardless of whether we can afford it or not, we may become ill and incur medical expenses. We cannot make money from air, but we can do our best to prepare for what is possible, given our circumstances.

As "Obamacare" rolls out in 2014, it should be possible for those who could not buy health insurance and/or could not afford insurance to find an insurance plan and, if below certain income levels, possibly to have help with the premiums. Pay attention to the details as they emerge and see if it is possible to find a way to be insured. No longer will insurance companies be able to cancel policies when we are in the middle of a healthcare crisis, and that should help families avoid finding themselves bankrupt because of healthcare costs, although it will not abolish all costs.

One last word. There is a distinction between quality of service and quality of care. In Houston, Ben Taub is a public hospital, used by the poor, the indigent, and those with no insurance. It can be crowded, chaotic, and slow, but it has great doctors, many of whom are also on the staff of the best private hospitals. It is the best place in the city to arrive by ambulance with severe trauma. The point is that good medical care is not guaranteed by the attractiveness of well-watered plants and fresh paint.

This is certainly true for hospice and nursing homes. All hospice care is covered by Medicare, but all hospices don't provide the same quality care. Nursing homes can be deceptive. Because a nursing facility or assisted living facility is fancy says nothing about the kind of care. A geriatric case manager of extensive experience urged one of her clients to look again more closely at a small family home provider that seemed "shabby" to the client but, in fact, provided good care at a significantly lower cost.

Note

The questions that head the following five chapters speak to paperwork related to death and dying. Preparing documents it is wise to have in place is more than just filling out forms. To fill out these forms, we have to admit to ourselves, at least for a moment, that we may die, and in engaging with paper, we are also engaging with emotions. We get double benefit.

If you have homes in more than one state, consider having forms for each state that conform to the laws of that state. Keep your documents accessible. It's a good idea to have a folder with all of your papers kept visible in your office or kitchen, a place where not only you but other family members can find them. But it is also helpful to have them stored online where you can access them if you are away. If you use Dropbox or cloud storage, you can scan copies of your forms and save them on these sites. Alternatively, you can slip a small pen drive into a purse or briefcase or on your key chain that will hold all your documents. Or you can use the old-fashioned way and just make several copies, perhaps leaving one set with children, friends or advisors.

Excellent tools to help prepare for completing forms and having conversations with both family and physicians are The Conversation Project's starter kits. You will find a starter kit in both English and Spanish for talking with family and a second kit for talking with physicians at www.conversationproject. org/starter-kit/intro.

See page 85 for a summary of forms and where to find them online. A more detailed discussion follows for each kind of form.

7. Why Do We Need a Healthcare Proxy Form Now?

It is easy to write that *now* is the time to put your end-of-life paperwork in order. But without a personal sense of urgency, odds are that you, like two thirds of Americans, will procrastinate. I want to impart that sense of urgency and then show you how you can do this paperwork at home easily without expense.

It is so hard to imagine being sick or injured and unable to speak for ourselves. It doesn't seem real. Here are two stories, old stories but still important, that underscore how real, in a minute, it can be. Many of you have heard of the cases of Karen Ann Quinlan and Terry Schiavo. Both were young women who collapsed into persistent vegetative states. It happened in the blink of an eye. Quinlan was twenty-one, Schiavo twenty-six. These were healthy young women who never expected to become incapacitated.

Karen Ann Quinlan, just recently turned twenty-one, became ill at a party. Her friends brought her home and put her to bed. When they checked fifteen minutes later, she was not breathing. Although they immediately called 911, Quinlan never returned to consciousness. After several months of medical intervention, her parents asked the hospital to remove the ventilator that was keeping their daughter alive, return her to her "natural state" and allow her, if it was the will of God, to die. Their daughter had left no written directions and the Quinlans, devout Catholics, looked to their church for guidance. The state, however, opposed their wishes; the county prosecutor threatened to bring homicide charges against the hospital if the ventilator was removed. After traumatic wrangling, the New Jersey Supreme Court ruled that the ventilator and feeding tube could be removed. Her parents removed the ventilator but continued feeding. Quinlan lived on another nine years, in a persistent vegetative state, before dying from pneumonia in 1985.

Terry Schiavo collapsed in 1990 and suffered massive brain damage from lack of oxygen. She had, as with most young people, no healthcare proxy that indicated who should speak for her in a medical crisis if she could not speak for herself nor an advance directive giving her wishes for treatment in writing. For several years, doctors tried to bring her back to consciousness. Finally, her husband Michael, who had, with the support of her parents, been appointed her guardian, asked the court to give him the right to remove her feeding tube. He needed court approval because he was opposed by her parents and did not have legal authorizations from his wife. In the absence of written documentation about what kind of care Terry would have chosen for herself, the courts had to resolve the issue. The litigation was long and ugly. Fifteen years after Terry Ann first fell unconscious, the feeding tube was removed, and Schiavo died shortly after in 2005.

Both cases are complicated (Wikipedia, which I used for these summaries, offers good reporting on both cases),[20] and laws have changed since they occurred. The reason for telling you these sad stories is to demonstrate that the unlikely is not impossible and to show how much controversy and disharmony can follow in the absence of legally acceptable documentation to provide medical guidance.

These two cases are famous. There are thousands of others that never reach the newspapers but create needless conflict. One of them happened to a woman I knew well. In her eighties, she fell ill and was hospitalized. Her two daughters, living in other states, flew to their mother's bedside while doctors tried this and that intervention. Their mother was conscious at the start but confused, and her daughters needed to make medical decisions. Neither had the written authority to act on her behalf. They both deeply loved their mother. One loved her so much she wanted everything possible done to save her. She demanded the doctors do more and more. The other loved her mother so much that she couldn't stand to see her suffer at her doctors' hands with no discernable results. She thought it was time to stop. The daughters were stressed, scared, and confused. Each night, they would go back to their mother's apartment and scream at each other. When their mother died, they stopped speaking and have not spoken since. Their mother, who never discussed her own ideas about when to stop rescue efforts, would have hated this even more than dying.

Documentation is easy. It is mostly free. It can be done without getting out of your pajamas. Once you have thought about what you want, you can complete the documentation at the breakfast table, in your bed, on your lunch break. All you need to do is go online, call up the necessary forms, complete them, print them, and ask two colleagues to witness them. It won't cost you anything. If your state requires notarization, that is one extra step. Frequently, someone in your work place or your bank can do the notarization. *Only legal paperwork counts.*

Start this paperwork by completing a form for a healthcare proxy, often included as part of the medical power of attorney. This form tells the world whom you want to speak for you if, in a healthcare situation, you can't speak for yourself. Best idea is to have a first choice and then a second and even a third in case the first choice is not able or available when you need this kind of help. You can change your mind at any time and redo the form with different names or revoke authority verbally, from the hospital bed if you wish.

If you are able to make your own decisions, then your proxy has no legal say. But what if you can't communicate, even if it's just for a short amount of time, and the doctors are looking for direction? Without direction, medical professionals usually opt for aggressive treatment. Decision-making around possible death can be complicated and confusing. Different family members have different ideas. Even different doctors have different ideas.

Dr. Nuland writes in *How We Die* of an unconscious selfishness that influences decision-making for a dying person. Everyone intends to what is best for the dying person. In fact, each family member and each doctor comes to a decision based on what seems best from his or her own point of view.

The challenge for many of us is that we are not ourselves sure, in the abstract, of what we are going to want. That's why we need a healthcare proxy who knows us well, who understands our values, who is willing to speak for us instead of himself. We need someone who will not wilt in the pressure of the moment and will ask the doctors to explain, communicate, and listen. And the only way that can happen is if we talk to this person when we write his or her name on our legal form. One place to find help deciding how to make your choices is the online California Advance Healthcare Directive Kit (http://www.sharingyourwishes. org/11_faq.asp).

Without a written form, most states stipulate that one's spouse, then one's adult children, then one's parents can speak for the person who cannot speak—but in some states no family member has legal authority. Having a legal document that gives evidence that you specifically authorize this person offers added weight to this voice. And if you know that someone who is not a family member will make better decisions for you, unless you have completed the paperwork in the proper way, that person may have no say.

This may sound strong to you, but I believe it is cruel to appoint someone as your proxy and not talk with him or her or, worse, never tell this person. You don't have to be specific about every decision that might have to be made. Many of us are not at all sure what to say. But we can talk through what we are thinking now and how we imagine we might make decisions given various scenarios. There are excellent websites with videos that let you role-play in your mind and help with conversation.[21] The American Bar Association has a Healthcare Proxy Quiz that you and your designated proxy (or proxies) should work through individually and then compare answers.[22] If you know you have been appointed to serve as someone's healthcare proxy, download the proxy quiz today and make sure each of you completes it and discusses the results. If you can't do it in person, use the phone, Skype, or email.

Since each state has its own form, some but not all of which are recognized by other states, it is best to use the form approved by your state. If you spend time in more than one state, complete a form for each state.

8. Why Complete An Advance Directive Now?

You may be too sick to talk. Maybe you are unconscious, have a tube in your throat, or have just emerged woozy from surgery. Whatever the reason, you are not the best person to be giving the medical team directions.

If there is no advance directive, also known as a medical power of attorney or a living will, that provides guidance about our wishes in the face of a terminal illness, we are likely to receive the most aggressive treatment, even if the chances of it helping us are very small and the odds of it leaving us severely compromised are great. The advance directive allows us to have a say about how to go forward.

The advance directive is specifically for end-of-life situations. If doctors believe our medical situation is terminal and we are likely to die in the coming six months, this document allows us to have a say in our treatment: do we want to stop treatment for recovery and provide only comfort care, or do we want the doctors to continue with all the methods they have at hand? Here is the opportunity to provide general instructions. For example, we might say that we want treatment to continue, but that we do not want a feeding tube or a ventilator or we do not want to be on a ventilator beyond a trial period to be decided by our healthcare proxy in consultation with our doctor.

A Do Not Resuscitate Order (DNR) is a particular form of advance directive. It only means that a person not be resuscitated if found with no pulse. Unfortunately, the advance directive and the more specific DNR can be misinterpreted. In a series of surveys by QuantiaMD, an online physician learning collaborative, many health professionals misunderstood the components of the advance directive. Often, physicians do not know the code status (i.e., whether or not there is a DNR in place) for their patients. Some would defibrillate a patient against orders and many would apply advance directive orders in circumstances that were not necessarily terminal. Having a legal document in hand, even taped to the door, helps us get the treatment we wish. But no paper will substitute for having direct communication with those men and women providing care.

One study found that in responses from medical residents and faculty at training institutions in thirty-four states, seventy-four percent of family physicians, seventy-seven percent of internists, and eighty percent of emergency room physicians misinterpreted advance directives and thought they were DNRs. To some, DNRs mean, incorrectly, providing less treatment. Is this alarming? Yes! Does it mean we should bypass having an advance directive? No! It means that we are wise to have a healthcare proxy or an advocate who knows us well and can step in and provide guidance. It means we should talk with our physicians the very next time we visit and ask them what we need to do to make our wishes clear if we find ourselves in a healthcare crisis. And talking about what we want once does not mean the conversation is over. Repetition helps, as does explaining our wishes to new doctors who may become involved in our care. It also means we should provide supplemental letters, which may be useful in bringing more clarity to situations that are seldom black or white.

It also means appreciating that we do the best we can, make the most rational decisions, communicate where and when it is possible, and then understand that sometimes, things happen. Sometimes they happen for the better; sometimes they don't. But the consensus of experts seems to be that we must work on educating healthcare professionals to use end-of-life documents properly and encourage patients to provide them.[23]

There is now yet another set of initials, AND. This stands for Allow Natural Death, and some prefer it Do Not Resuscitate, thinking it sounds less harsh for both patients and family members. However, there is not now common agreement about what is "natural." The DNR gives clear direction and, for now, it is the term I use.

Different states have different advance directive forms. It is important to use the form for the state in which you claim primary residence. If you live in more than one state, it is a good idea to fill out forms for each state. The number of pages you find varies by state and from where you download the form. For Texas, my state, there are seventeen pages from one source, but these include helpful instructions. For Kansas, there are only five pages; for Hawaii, eleven. However, the form itself is only two pages.

No matter how many pages come out of the computer, this is not difficult to complete so don't be discouraged. Completing an advance directive is a tool to help us start thinking about what may make sense for us at the end of life.

It can be hard to decide what we want. One way to move toward clarity is to purchase a small booklet, *Five Wishes*, from the *Aging With Dignity* website or download it at no cost from fivewishesonline.agingwithdignity.org/ and go through the five questions it poses, with different choices, with a friend or family member. This short pamphlet comes in twenty-seven languages and costs five dollars. Our Death, Dying and Dessert group has helped all of us who participate to get clearer about what we want by listening to others, by listening to ourselves, and just by thinking about the questions. Talk. Talking about dying may be one of our last taboos, but as with other forbidden topics, when we let them out in the sunlight, they become less scary and less confusing. I have changed my own ideas and feel smarter about this subject since I started these conversations. It doesn't feel morbid. It feels good.

Understand that the advance directive does not deal with all the shades of grey that arise in a healthcare crisis. It points in a direction but does not address the many "what ifs" and 'how mights" that happen in real life. It is designed to provide guidance when we are already in the hospital and in a crisis. There is a new document now being used that gives direction on what to do while we are still at home. It addresses whether or not to take us to a hospital, whether we want cardiopulmonary resuscitation (CPR) in the hospital or outside the hospital, how we feel about artificial nutrition and antibiotics, and where we want to die.

This new document is called a POLST (Physicians Orders for Life Sustaining Treatment) or MOLST (Medical Orders for Life Sustaining Treatment). These are not patient instructions. They are written doctors' orders, not patient orders. In states that require these forms, men and women with chronic or life-limiting illness or advanced age are interviewed by a physician or a physician's representative. Both the patient and the doctor (or in some states other medical personnel) sign the form, and it goes into one's medical chart. You might post it on your refrigerator as well. At the end of 2012, only thirteen states require a POLST, but at least that many have developing programs. More information about the POLST is available at http://dying.about.com/od/ethicsandchoices/f/POLST.htm.

Once you do all the paperwork, you are entitled to applause, but you are on pause, not on stop. Every decade, revisit all your paperwork. The common wisdom says the time to review this is in the face of one of five Ds: decade, divorce, diagnosis, decline, or a death. You might decide that every five years after age sixty-five, you will do a review of your thinking and make sure your paperwork is aligned with your thoughts.

9. Why Do Most People Benefit From Making A Will Now?

You may think you have not written a will, but the reality is that you already have a will even if you have not done a thing about it. All of us are subject to the default directive that each state puts in place for those who die intestate, which is the legal term for dying without a will. If you die intestate, the state will appoint an executor, often a friend of the judge's, and your estate will pay fees for this person as well as for a bond, an inventory, and accounting. This executor must distribute what you own following a formula set by the state. If you have minor children, the state will decide who should be their guardian rather than you.

I was once doing a radio show, and a listener called in to talk about his aunt who died with no will and about forty thousand dollars in total assets. "Just about everything went to cover the legal costs because she didn't want to pay a lawyer while she was alive," he said. "You are right, lady, in telling everyone to have a will."

This section is written with the hope of moving you forward into executing a will if you don't already have one. Perhaps you are thinking, "Wait a minute, you don't know anything about me or my circumstances so how do you get off telling me I need to make a will?" I may not know you, but here is what I *do* know. Since only thirty percent of Americans have wills, odds are you don't have one. If you don't, there is a good chance you believe one or more of the following:

- I don't own enough to worry about a will.
- Everything I own will go to my spouse, so I don't need a will.
- It's too expensive.
- I'm going to do it, but there is no hurry. I am in good health and am not old.
- Making a will is risking fate. I'm not even going to imagine I'll need one.

Making a will does not incur ill fortune, or else the thirty percent who have completed their wills would have an exceptionally high death rate. Rather, it protects you against unexpected crises.

Who certainly needs a will?

- If you have children under age eighteen. You will need a will that is clear about guardianship. Make provisions for what happens if the other parent is unable to assume guardianship, or you are divorced, have custody, and don't feel the other biological parent would be a suitable parent.
- If you own more than a house and a car, both with deeds that specify a successor owner, a joint bank account, and maybe a retirement fund with a designated

beneficiary. Remember that everything in your house is part of your estate.

- If you have children from a previous relationship.
- If you are separated but not divorced.
- If you are living together but not married.
- If you are a same sex unmarried couple.
- If you want someone other than your spouse and/ or children to inherit, or if you want to specify who receives what and how much.
- If there is any chance family members will disagree.

A very good website posted by a law firm in Gloucester City, NJ, Puff and Cockerill, asks and answers the question Why Do I Need a Will? It's an excellent summary of who does and who does not need a will and why (http://www.pufflaw.com/).

Almost always our affairs are more complicated than we realize. It is simpler for those we leave behind if we do have a will. But maybe you are confident things are completely uncomplicated. You are young or old and don't own much. You are married and everything is jointly owned and there are no children. You are single and think there will be no family issues. I am going to provide some online lowcost options for people who believe they do not need a will or cannot afford a lawyer just now. But heed the cautions of an estate attorney with thirty years of experience:

People think their affairs are simple, and we discover that they are not. They use computer forms and don't complete them accurately, and they are invalid. They use forms or make provisions not accepted in the state where they live. They don't get required notarization. They forget a small account that causes the estate to need court action. They write out a holographic will and use language that doesn't fit their circumstances. The majority of people are well served by visiting a lawyer and having a will drawn up for them.

Here is an option for people whose affairs appear simple or who feel they cannot afford an estate attorney just now: consider an online will preparation service. Among the choices are LegacyWriter.com and BuildaWill.com, which will walk you through a questionnaire and insert your answers into a will for $19.95, or Quicken WillMaker Plus for $39.99. LegalZoom.com, which also starts with a questionnaire, will then have a "specialist," who is not necessarily a lawyer, review your answers for completeness, starting at $69. Each state has different rules for wills, so any legitimate form or service must be tailored to your state as the online forms usually are. If you can afford a few hundred dollars to visit a lawyer, complete the form and ask to have it reviewed for you. You can ask about cost up front.

If you decide it is time to visit an estate attorney (i.e., a lawyer who specializes in inheritance issues), consider investing in just one more book before you go: Elizabeth Arnold's *Creating The Good Will: The Most Comprehensive Guide to Both the Financial and Emotional Sides of Passing on Your Legacy.*

Arnold's book is simply terrific. She calls herself a "crisis prevention coach" and turns the estate planning process upside down, believing we should focus first on the human issues and then move to the technical, legal, and financial structures that best address them.

This book does not explain all the various ins and outs of taxes, trusts, and other instruments available to us. The reason we visit with an estate attorney is to understand how best to write a will in ways that make sense for our particular situation. What Arnold's book does, something that estate attorneys rarely have time to do, is prepare you to write your will in the context of your values, your family, your hopes and wishes for the future.

10. Why Is It a Good Idea to Have a Financial Power of Attorney?

We talked above about the advance directive or medical power of attorney. That document gives a person you name the right to make medical decisions on your behalf when you cannot. This document gives someone you select the right to make financial decisions on your behalf.

I've talked with older adults who have no wish for their children to know about their finances. Putting a financial power of attorney in place does not mean you have to tell your kids how much money you have or where you spend it. It does mean that if you are unable to pay your bills, make investment decisions, sign business documents, pay your taxes, or take care of other financial matters, someone you have authorized, who is legally obligated to act with your best interests in mind and keep good records, is there to act for you.

"Well, I've got my wife to do that," a seventy-five-year-old retired company president explains to me. And, indeed, for many things he does. In our house, I am the person designated to deal with financial paperwork and, in most cases, I already have authorization to do so. But just before

I sat down to write this section, I hit a bump. My husband's Required Minimum Distribution check, the amount of money the government requires he withdraw from an employer retirement plan, did not arrive as expected. When it hit me that we didn't have that check, I called the company that managed the retirement account. Although I have a specific power of attorney on the accounts there, I was told I didn't have it on the 401k account (although subsequent conversations revealed that this was incorrect, but I had no way to prove it at the moment.) I was unable to check up on this check. Happily, my husband was only out swimming, not incapacitated. Were he unable to talk, I would have needed to have on file a durable power of attorney form to send the company to allow them to talk with me, which is hard to get from someone who is incapacitated, or involve the court system.

If property, bank accounts, or business ownership are in one name only, our spouses or children have no right to act on our behalf without a power of attorney form. There is a distinction it helps to understand. A durable power of attorney is one that endures or lasts without regard to events until you die. You can also create a limited power of attorney for a specific activity that is meant to be time-limited. For example, you are going in for surgery and an important business matter may occur while you are in surgery or recovering and unable to conduct business. You can authorize someone to act on your behalf but specify that this permission expires at a given time or is made obsolete by a given event.

It's a good idea to have, as with your healthcare proxy, someone who is named first and then someone who is named second. Suppose Michael and I are in an accident together and someone needs to pay our bills until we are able. The person who has our medical power of attorney (healthcare proxy) does not need to be the same person who has our financial power of attorney. And neither need be related to us.

The power of attorney form is only good while we are living. When we die, the executor of our estate becomes the person who handles our affairs. As discussed in Chapter 8, if there is no will and no executor appointed, the state is going to appoint one, and our estate is going to pay that person.

In many families, money matters are regarded as private. Talking about money is taboo, and telling your children about your financial situation is unacceptable. Sometimes, it's because we fear our children will be grasping if they know all of our assets. Sometimes, it is because we have tried to appear as if we have more assets then we do, and we don't want our kids to worry or pity us. There may be good reasons for remaining private about our financial affairs, but there are good reasons for being forthcoming as well. If a spouse or child is going to have to step in and take charge, it is helpful for them not to be blindsided but rather have some understanding of the whole financial picture. If you think you can earn loyalty and attention with the expectation of an inheritance that is not in the cards, you are dealing in deception, and the issues are not financial but emotional. You might want to see if you can address these while you are able.

There are ways to talk about our resources without being dollar specific. You might say, "I want you to know where we have accounts and the name of the person there who helps me," without revealing how much is in the account. You might want to make sure both your name and your spouse's name are on accounts and deeds. You might want to make sure you have a succession agreement in place with business partners. If you have secret stashes, you need to be sure someone will be able to locate and access them. I know of a man who keeps large amounts of cash in a safe deposit box. It is a secret from his family and his government. Only he has the key to the box. No one else's name is on the box. Unless he intends for that money, one day, to be turned over to the government as unclaimed property, someone will need to know it is there.

It is possible to download a free power of attorney form or, perhaps, secure one from your bank. If you plan to visit an estate attorney to complete a will, ask your attorney to provide this form and advise you if it needs to be customized. Otherwise, consider paying twenty dollars and using the online form from TotalLegal.com. I like this form because it asks you specifically to check what authorizations you give to the person to whom you grant your power of attorney. These include the following:

- ☐ Check all powers.
- ☐ Real estate—Manage, sell, and buy real estate.
- ☐ Personal property—Manage, sell, and buy personal property such as cars and furniture.
- ☐ Stock and bond transactions—Purchase, sell, and exchange stocks, bonds, and mutual funds.
- ☐ Commodities and option transactions—Buy, sell, and exercise options and commodities.
- ☐ Banking and other financial transactions—Manage a wide array of banking activities including paying bills, managing bank accounts and credit cards.
- ☐ Business operation—Operate a business.
- ☐ Insurance—Manage, create, or terminate insurance policies.
- ☐ Estate or trust beneficiary matters—Manage activities regarding an estate or trust for a specific beneficiary.
- ☐ Claims/litigation—Handle or initiate any claims or litigation.
- ☐ Personal and family maintenance—Maintain the normal standard of living.
- ☐ Social Security, Medicare, and Medicaid benefits—Manage program benefits.
- ☐ Retirement plans—Manage retirement plans.
- ☐ Tax matters—Prepare tax returns, manage tax payments or refunds.
- ☐ Property transfers—Make any property transfers required to qualify the person granting the power of attorney to qualify for medical care assistance programs.
- ☐ Make Gifts of property—Make gifts of real estate and personal property.

You can check any of these or not. You can also use this form to appoint a guardian for your person if necessary. Do remember that the form needs to be notarized and, in some states, witnessed. If an attorney is not supervising the notarization, consider using your bank.

11. Should We Donate Our Organs?

The National Network of Organ Donors explains on its website why the decision to donate and willingness to document that decision can matter dramatically to someone:

> The Problem: Tragically, 19 people die every day in this country waiting for an organ transplant. At The National Network of Organ Donors, we believe that number should be zero—and we are dedicated to ensuring that every single person in the U.S. who needs a transplant gets one.
>
> The statistics are staggering — and heartbreaking. More than 111,000 people are currently on UNOS' transplant waiting list, and the number of people who die waiting for transplants continues to grow: from 10 people each day in 1990, to 14 a day in 1996, to 19 today. That number will be even higher by 2020 unless we make a serious effort to reverse the trend today.
>
> The problem isn't that people don't want to donate organs or even that they don't sign up to become donors. It's that currently the healthcare and legal systems don't

ensure that a person's wishes regarding organ donation are honored. Even if you sign a donor card or the back of your driver's license, if your family doesn't give its approval, the hospital will not procure your organs—in spite of your prior written consent. The National Network of Organ Donors believes that signing a legal document should guarantee, without exception, that your wishes are met.

The best way to sign up to donate organs, tissue or eyes is do so online:

http://www.thenationalnetworkoforgandonors.org/register.php

This form puts you in the donor bank nationally. If you don't use a computer, you can contact The National Network of Organ Donors, Inc. by calling 866 577-9798 or writing them in Florida at PO Box 223613, West Palm Beach, FL 33422.

Once you have signed up to donate, you can help others know of your decision by having the donation noted on your driver's license, telling your family members, putting a copy of your donation form in your medical chart, and adding a note to your advance directive. Cancer patients cannot donate, and age and lingering illness can prevent donation, but when we complete the donation form now, we make donation a possibility for the future.

Many people who need an organ transplant are now using living donors, often family members or close friends. Visit www.mytransplantlife.com or www.transplant.org for more information.

If you have questions about donating, visit http://www. organdonor.gov/lifestories/lifeheight.html. You can read the stories of some donor recipients there as well. And if you want to know more about the ethics of organ donation and the reasons for the shortage of organs, visit the Hastings Center website.[24]

Forms Summary

If you visit the Y Collaborative website (www.ycollaborative. com) and look under the Resources section, you can access the forms discussed here. Here is a summary of the forms you are being urged to complete and where to download them on the Internet. An estate attorney can also provide you with these forms and help you execute them. And once you have completed them, remember to revisit and review when there are major changes in your life or every ten years to be sure you are conforming to current laws and account for any changes in your circumstances. Place your documents where they can be accessed quickly.

1. **Healthcare Proxy**, also known as the Healthcare Agent or Medical Power of Attorney, which gives legal power to another person to speak on your behalf when you cannot.

2. **Advance Directive**, also known as a Living Will or Medical Power of Attorney, which provides directions for what kind of treatment you want if doctors believe you have six months or less to live. Go to the Caring Connections website (www.caringinfo.org). Click on Planning Ahead. On the right side of the screen, in a box at the top, you will see a box that says "Free Downloads. State Specific Advance Directives." This will take you to forms for your state for the healthcare proxy (Healthcare Agent) and the advance directive. There is lots of explanation here as well.

3. **Do Not Resuscitate Order (DNR)**, which prevents medical personnel from doing CPR (chest compressions or electrical stimuli to restart a heart that has stopped

beating). People who want DNRs may need both in-hospital and outofhospital forms. Ask your doctor for a form or type "DNR form for (name your state)" into your Internet browser.

4. **POLST,** Physician Orders for Life Sustaining Treatment (alternatively called MOLST, Medical Orders for Life Sustaining Treatment, in some states), which is a doctor-signed order for your medical record explaining your wishes for endof-life decisions. It is intended specifically for frail elderly who are likely to die in the near future. A sample form can be found at MDS30ApprovedPOLSTForm.pdf or Google "POLST form." These forms are not used in all states, but the purpose of the form is relevant for all frail elderly.

5. **A Will,** which is a legal document that instructs the court about who should inherit what you own and how, who should oversee your estate, and who, if you have minor children, should be their guardian. For simple wills, go to LegacyWriter.com and BuildaWill.com, Quicken WillMaker Plus at nolo.com or LegalZoom. com. A simple free form can be found at Onlinelegal. com.

6. **Financial Power of Attorney,** which gives legal power to someone else to act on your behalf regarding legal and financial matters when you cannot. These powers can be limited by your directions. You can find free power of attorney forms for each state online, but I prefer the TotalLegal form, which costs $19.95 online but walks you through the different kinds of powers

you may or may not wish to assign to the person to whom you are granting the right to act legally on your behalf. Visit TotalLegal.com. It may be wise to work with an estate attorney in designing this form, which can be helpful but also dangerous in the wrong hands.

7. **Organ Donation Form** which provides legal proof that you wish to donate organs or tissue. To register for organ donation, go to http://www.thenationalnetworkoforgandonors.org/register.php.

8. **Supplemental Letter**, which clarifies your thinking. Write whatever you wish to help explain your feelings and the process you hope will be used if others must make decisions for you at the end of your life.

9. **Medications List and Doctor Contacts**, which provide quick access to what medications you take and who has followed your medical care. Keep a list in your wallet. For online storage, you can use Dropbox or other online storage programs that are available to you from any computer for all documents. One helpful way to organize your medications is to use the government's My Medical Records form. Just type the name into your Internet browser.

A website that appeared just as I was finishing the draft of this book, *Prepare*, offers very basic, simple information about end-of-life preparation. The material can be read or can be seen and listened to in movie form. It was written by academic physicians but designed to be understood by people with as little as a fifth-grade education. Visit www.prepareforyourcare.org.

12. Why Add a Supplemental Letter or Make a Video?

Let's say that you are one of those rare organized people. You have all your paperwork in place: a healthcare proxy form, an advance directive, a power of attorney, a will, a list of medications, a list of professionals who help you, and still other lists you think advisable. Surely you are *done*?

Almost. If you have not talked with your family or those closest to you, you are not done. The forms are informative but not personal. This very last step is to add the personal touch, to reach out with your voice and say what only you can say. You can say these things in person, but one way to make sure that the conversation has staying power is to write a letter, make a tape, shoot a video. Conversation at the dinner table can be can be terrific but, with very good fortune, you don't die for another ten or twenty years. And since it may feel to you like you just had a conversation, you don't have another one.

All the forms urged on you in this book are critically important for legal reasons. They can also ease decision-making for both family and physician. But they are just paper. It is in the nature of forms to be unambiguous even if the situation to which they must be applied is not black or white. Yes, if I know I am likely to die in six months, I want you to stop treatment, or I want you to continue treatment. Sometimes, it really is that clear. But often—and we all know this—life gets blurry.

A supplemental letter, tape, or video is intended to do the following:

- Give those who will be worrying about you some help in figuring out how you want them to think in this crisis. This is a place to say, "I understand how difficult this can be. Here are some of the criteria that, as I write this now, seem useful to me."

- Offer them understanding. In the event that they do what they think is right and later, after you have left this earth, they worry that they made a mistake, your letter is a chance to assure them that you understood how difficult this all was, how there may have been no right answer, and that they should let go and move on.

- Leave a legacy of love. This is the place to write "I love you" and elaborate with whatever good things you can say. The refusal of important people in our lives to exit stage right with compassion and forgiveness haunts many of us long after their death.

This is not the place to settle scores, remind people of their failings, or score a last dig. This is the place to show up as your best self since that self will remain in place long after you have departed.

If you find writing difficult, talk into a tape recorder or get a friend to record a video of you on something as simple as a smart phone.

Our letters will reflect our values and beliefs, our personalities, and our hopes. I am sharing with you my letter to my sons not because I think it is a model for anyone else but because, perhaps, it helps to see what something like this could look like. Mine is long because I like to write, but length is not a requirement. In Appendix III you will find letters written by others. If you like any of what you find, take it. If you dislike it, bounce up against it to figure out what you want to say. Write what makes sense for you. Yours can be short. It can be a list or phrases. The writing is not important. It is the gift of your thinking and feeling that matters.

Supplemental Letter

Dear Jonathan and Seth,

In just about a month, I will have a sixty-ninth birthday. In the context of holding contradictions (a skill the modern world seems to require more and more), I see this as an age that, really, is in the category of old and yet, at the same time, isn't so old – and I don't just mean on the inside. Dad and I are in this wonderful time of our lives. Our glorious month in NYC had us walking three to six miles a day, up and down the subway steps and feeling pretty carefree. We have great pleasure in being with each other. We are delighted by you and the good women you have married and by our grandchildren. It is a good life that fills me with gratitude. But I am clear that it does not go on endlessly, and it will not, mostly likely, continue without difficulties. Something bad will happen. I say this not because I am a pessimist but a realist. It's what happens.

With all the pleasures and satisfactions life has so fortunately brought me over many years, I will not die too young. But, of course, I will certainly die too soon, too soon to find out the end of the next story, whatever it might be...to watch the grandchildren graduate or marry or begin this or that, to watch you move with curiosity into your own next stages.

As you know, beginning with Nana's decline on the cusp of 2008 to her death towards the end of 2010, I became interested in death and dying and have been studying it and talking about it since. One thing I have learned, both from my own experiences with Nana and from the literature, is that our fear of talking about death does not make things easier. It makes them, I believe, harder.

It is impossible to know what I will feel when faced with death as a reality. Maybe I will find out what I have thought before was wrong and want to revise all this,...but I'm going to bet that much of what I am thinking will, in fact, be helpful. In every other aspect of my life, thinking about choices and decisions in advance turned out to have been a good idea. And, wearing my mother hat, I want to help you as well in what will be a difficult time. Here is another contradiction: I hope you will want to hang on to me forever and yet be willing to say goodbye and let me go when it is time. This is work we each must do.

I have two fears. The first is that I will find myself in a circumstance in which my brain is so devastated by dementia or trauma that I am not aware of my environment and cannot respond to the people I love but others may force me to exist in a prolonged state of dependence and indignity; or a circumstance in which my brain is intact but there is no reasonable hope that my body will even function normally and others may force me to endure unnecessary pain and/or suffering when withholding food and fluids and/or providing only comfort care would allow me to die. Know that I think hospice is a terrific thing and those with terminal conditions in hospice programs seem to live longer than terminally ill patients in full-bore rescue treatment.

The second fear is that my instructions to my medical proxy and my doctor to avoid invasive medical procedures including intubation, ventilator, and feeding tube will be misunderstood and so avoided in circumstances that require only short-term intervention to return me to a satisfactorily (ah, and if I cannot, you are going to have to imagine what I would find satisfactory) functional state. I guess I have a third fear. I am afraid of pain. It scares me more than death.

I am not afraid to die. I am afraid that the needs and values of others will trump my own desires to be allowed to end my life in the manner I choose. If there is confusion on the part of physicians about how to treat me, I hope this supplement to my advance directive will provide sufficient guidance. Of course, if dad is here and able, he is my healthcare proxy. If this is not a choice, then I have designated Jonathan to take on this role. As I explained when we completed the legal documents, I thought it would be easier (if not easy) for Jonathan to deal with this than Seth. If Jonathan cannot do this, then Seth, you are on first. If your father must bear this responsibility, I hope this letter will make it easier for you to support him. My friend and partner in Y Collaborative, Nancy Rust, knows as well as anybody my feelings in this area and can be a source of advice if needed.

If ANY of the following conditions apply and are likely to continue to apply going forward, I do not wish any form of life support or invasive treatment, and if I am not in a hospital, I do not wish to be admitted to one but sent to a hospice or provided comfort care at home:

I cannot recognize the people I love.

I cannot recall the essence of the person I was or the life I led in terms of its fundamental values or significant events.

I cannot communicate my wishes by words, gestures, or sounds.

I am not aware of my environment through my senses so I cannot respond.

I cannot make meaningful plans to change my environment.

I am totally dependent on others or machines for nurturance, or I do not have the mental ability to know how to eat or drink, or I actively resist attempts to feed me.

I seem extremely confused or scared, seem to be living in horror.

I seem to harbor delusions that lead to behavior dangerous enough to require constraint.

I am extremely withdrawn, apathetic, despondent, irritable, or angry, even after I have received treatment attempts to improve my mood.

I am incontinent, cannot accept it, and will continue with no expectation of relief in such a state of indignity.

I have intense pain or unbearable suffering that can only be alleviated by medications that sedate me so much I can hardly be aroused.

The burdens of treatment to maintain my existence have become my or my caregivers' overwhelming concern and threaten to bring significant financial harm to my family.

However, if circumstances place me in any one of more of these conditions for a brief amount of time with strong likelihood that the circumstance will end, and I can return to living a life of cognition with the possibility of pleasures still, then I probably prefer treatment—but I am not really sure even of that. The likelihood of a return to functioning well must be significant and improvement must be demonstrated. Futile treatment is of no value, even if it may bring benefit to others. While you will need to apply independent judgment to the particulars of a given situation, and I appreciate that, never choose a difficult treatment only to gain a few months of life. In the face of death, get out of the way. Do not hesitate to withhold hydration and nutrition to facilitate a death that is waiting in the wings. And know that whatever you decide, I know you will be acting with intelligence and compassion and a desire to do as I wished, so do not second guess yourselves. Mistakes will be made. Death is messy and there is no good script. Do the best you can and stop!

I know from Nana how difficult it is to see someone in a life-threatening circumstance and not to want rush in and try to save the person. You may have to steel yourselves to resist this very human impulse. Understand that death is not, I believe, the worst thing that can happen. If you find yourself faced with a crisis and know you should not call the hospital, call hospice, ask for a hospice nurse, and sit with me, hold me, love me. Do not be afraid to let me die. It will be a gift of incredible love to be able to do this…and if you find, in a moment, that you cannot, forgive yourself.

If it is possible to donate any organs—perhaps my organs will age out—certainly do that.

I prefer to be cremated. Let's think about what to do with the ashes as I still have Nana's ashes on our bookshelves. We don't want to be a family of three generations of ashes. So, I think you could sprinkle them by the ocean in California. Seth, perhaps you may want to do your sprinkling in Rhode Island. It makes no difference. Return me to the earth. And have a party. Celebrate a life well lived. My only stipulation is that the food be really good. If there is enough money to do so and you can all agree, you might all go somewhere wonderful and do the celebrating. But do celebrate. There is so much to celebrate!

A parent's illness and dying do strange things to family. I know this from what happened to David and me and from ample literature discussion. Don't fight childhood battles. I didn't love Jonathan more than Seth or Seth more than Jonathan. You both, in equal measure it seems, drove me nuts and delighted me. You are both wonderful men, good husbands, good fathers, and completely delicious sons. If you need to hire someone to help settle the estate, just do it and pay them. I expect whenever Dad and I die, both of you will be fully engaged in a busy adulthood. Don't fight over stuff. It is only stuff. Help all the grandkids get what they need and pay to ship it to them wherever they need it. Let your wives choose what they might be able to use in your homes. Do it in rounds if necessary.

So, you already know I'm a bit odd. This may reinforce that perception, but I want to say something here that's unusual. I have told your father that if circumstances happen so that I am not who I used to be and cannot give love or receive love, but my body is still functioning, he has my encouragement to find a woman to whom to give love and from whom to receive love. Don't think negatively of him if this transpires. It is my wish…my command. Help him in this difficult place to be. And if I have dementia and don't seem to care about food, it is good to withhold nutrition and hydration. Living on and on this way is just nuts. You can't kill me—at least not at this writing—but you don't want to do all you can to prolong a life that is not a life.

One more thing. Nana taught me that we might think roles have been reversed and now we are parents to our parent. A child can never be parent to a parent. I think it was that sense that I was trying to be her parent that angered my mother. As the adult child of an aging parent, you do have to take on burdens and responsibilities. But you are not my parent and should not have that sense of responsibility. As accepting you as adults meant giving you the right to screw up your own lives, I hang on to that right forever.

Oh, yet still another thing. When the end of my life is near, if it is possible for us to talk, let's do that. Do not be afraid to talk about dying, to ask how I feel, and to tell me how you feel. You will, I imagine from my own experience, feel sadness and impatience and confusion and love and maybe even guilt and nostalgia. All normal. We have always spoken openly and directly. You know how much I value that. Please don't let dying get in the way of that. Keep talking from the heart and from the mind. Come into my bedroom and laugh, be your usual irreverent selves, and if Dad is still here, bring him along and help him. It will be very, very hard.

There is much written about leaving a legacy. I think the best legacy we can leave is a legacy of love, and that I leave to all of you…in abundance, with so much heart and happiness.

Susan A. Lieberman
7/9/11

13. What Other Information Do We Need In Place?

We need no excuse for being disorganized. It's like breathing… it happens. Most of us have better intentions about getting our paperwork together than we have actions. But there are some people who just have it together. My cousin, Jim Steinback, is one of those people. An engineer by training, a neatnik by temperament, Jim is uber-orderly.

In 2009, he put together for a couples group he belongs to what he calls The Croak Book, a complete summary of all the information we should provide before our death. I included much of it in my last book, *Getting Old Is A Full Time Job: Moving on from a Life of Working Hard,* but did not include the templates in Jim's original document. This time, I would like readers to have access to the entire document. In Appendix IV, you will find a URL that will take you to Jim's Croak Book. One caution: it is Jim's good fortune that he accumulated significant assets in his life, as have the others in his group. His book is written for people with more complicated and ample estates that most of us have. Just ignore what doesn't apply to you and take what does.

Here is the hard part: It is very likely you will look at his work and say, "Wow, this is great, and I need to do this." And then you won't. You might try this strategy: Get a binder or file folder. Label the empty sections. Print out the relevant sections and put them in the file folder. Then each week, do one section. Put a list in your date book and check off what is done. Better yet, do it in tandem with a good friend and hold each other accountable. Or take one weekend and power through. If you ever have been the executor for someone else's estate, you already know what a gift this kind of organization is to those who have to cope after you move on.

Additionally, if you are seriously ill, you may wish to consider the DNR form mentioned in Chapter 7. If this form has been filled out in the hospital and you return home, you need to have an out-of-hospital DNR form (OOHDNR.). Each state has its own forms.

A DNR is meant to prevent cardiopulmonary resuscitation from being administered if we stop breathing. Why would we want to stop CPR? The odds of it being successful are small, and the chances of it doing damage are significant, especially in elderly people when rapid chest pounding frequently leads to broken bones. CPR is helpful for less than five percent of elderly patients with multiple medical problems. It is useful in six to fifteen percent of hospital patients, but those figures don't tell us that many patients who leave the hospital never return to health. Outside the hospital, effectiveness varies from two to thirty percent. Obviously, if someone is healthy and in midlife, the chances of CRP working well are much better than if he or she is ill and old, but they are never as good as television would lead us to believe.[25] A recently published book *Erasing Death* by Sam Parnia, M.D., Ph.D. focuses on what we need to do to improve the results of CPR dramatically, even after people are considered technically dead.

If you do not want medical personnel who may be called to your home to attempt to rescue you with CPR, post your DNR on the refrigerator or on a door so it is readily available. But it's also useful to keep a copy with you in case you have an event that happens while you are at dinner with your family or shopping with a caretaker. If you do not want 911 responders to perform CPR and then bundle you up and take you to a hospital, you must have clear, legal instructions readily available.

We talked in the Advance Directive section, Chapter 8, about having a POLST or MOLST form if we are old and ill and expect life to end soon. This is a new form designed to help people who are failing to consider what they want and to prevent hospitals and nursing homes particularly from providing care that people do not wish.

It is a good idea for those of us who are over sixty-five, even if we feel quite young, to have our doctors' contact information and our daily medications in our wallets. In fact, it is a good idea for anyone. If we are in an accident and show up unable to communicate, a family member can quickly explain what drugs we have been taking and who prescribed them. The US Food and Drug Administration has put a form online called My Medicine Record that helps us organize what kinds of drug information we want to have at hand. The form is found at www.fda.gov/Drugs/ ResourcesForYou/ucm079489.htm.

Finally, where do we keep all our medical information? On the computer? That's fine but how about a file or box right in the kitchen or office readily seen and grabbed? How about in the cloud or on a pen drive in our possession so that if we are traveling, it can be located? A small card in our wallet with our meds is sensible.

Beyond the basics, I recently heard about a woman who knew her cancer was incurable. She spent time her last few years documenting all the important art, jewelry, and furniture in her house, typing up a little story about where each came from and why it was important. Another organized person put labels on art and in her jewelry box letting her grandchildren know the provenance of her pieces.

14. How Do We Start A Conversation About Death And Dying With Family And Friends?

"**P**olite people," my gracious southern friend insists, "do not discuss sex, religion, and politics and they don't, Susan, discuss dying either." But we do discuss sex. It seems we are discussing it everywhere. We might not like the way we discuss politics, but that, too, is everywhere. (Note: I am writing this sentence on Election Day 2012, so I feel particularly overdosed on politics.) We might not talk about what we think of someone else's religion in his or her presence, but it is another taboo that has bitten the dust as has weight, impotence, and depression. Heavens, if we can talk about all that, what's a little death and dying chatter?

It's good for our health to talk about death. Admitting that we will die can help us live more fully now. No postponing things we say are important but put off. No waiting for just the right moment to allow us to set good plans in motions. Seize the day because who knows when the day will seize us.

We want to talk to with our family or dear friends, with people who will have responsibility for our wellbeing if we are ill or die unexpectedly because:

- They need to know where our important papers are and who can help them if help is needed.
- They need to know what we think about medical care in a crisis.
- If we die, they deserve some guidance in planning our funeral and settling our estate.
- We need to make sure the people we love hear it from us and feel that love while we can deliver it. And we need to forgive those who may suffer without it.
- If we talk now, then it is likely it will be easier for others to talk to us when they need to speak frankly about difficult health issues.
- We can help others become more comfortable with the subject by our example and encourage them to put their own lives in order.

We know from dozens of reports that adult children may roll their eyes and try to resist discussing their own parents' possible deaths. It's such an unpleasant thought. And we know parents may resist, even refuse, to discuss end-of-life planning with their adult children. Experience suggests that most people, once lured into a conversation, are glad to have had it. We cannot force someone to talk if they are set against it. We can make a request and then explain that we are going to try again later, so please, do think about it.

Here are some ways to organize the conversation:

- **Ask for a conversation as a gift.** I asked my children, who happened to be in the same city for a birthday of mine, to give me an hour to discuss this as my birthday gift. A friend asked her parents to prepare their paperwork, including a will, and to discuss their thoughts with her as her Christmas gift.

- **Use a family gathering as time to start talking**. Alert people to your intention and ask them to give it a try. You may not want to do this over pumpkin pie at Thanksgiving dinner but you could suggest an hour in the afternoon or the next morning. Or you could schedule a dinner just for this purpose. If you are not averse to wine or beer, a bit of spirits can help conversations.

- **Use the *Five Wishes* brochure** to get people thinking and then talking. Ask the people you care about if they would talk about their reactions to the questions in the brochure as a way to help you figure out your own. (See *www.agingwithdignity.org/five-wishes*.)

- **Tell a story** that you know about or have read about in which a family was caught unprepared and it caused painful difficulties. These stories are all around us. My friend's husband, in his midfifties, flew off to Africa on a medical mission. He was overweight and had diabetes. The altitude in the mountains made him ill and before help could reach him, he was dead. He had no will, no insurance other than what his work place provided, and no directions for his wife about how to manage his estate. His death was a terrible blow to his family that was exacerbated by the absence of preparation.

The uncle of an acquaintance died without ever explaining to his second wife, his children and stepchildren, and his business partners how he decided to allocate his estate. Everyone blamed others for actions over which no one but the dead man had control.

Tell your story and explain that you do not want your own family to have difficulties because talking about the inevitable end of life seemed inappropriate or just difficult.

Perhaps you are reluctant to talk because you want to leave your assets in a way that you fear will make some members of your family unhappy. You want to avoid the pain of their displeasure so you say nothing. What most often happens is that others, those who benefitted from your death, suffer the pain of displeasure that should have been yours.

- **Use family giving as a way into talking.** If your family has a cause, charity, or organization to which it feels a commitment and, perhaps, has supported with gifts over time, you might talk with your children or younger family members about your wish to have this continue under their stewardship. Or if there is just something you care about—the local library, a neighborhood park, an animal care group—you might talk about how you wish to leave a legacy to this cause. Beginning there can be a road in to a more intimate conversation of death and dying and how you hope your family will respond.

A neutral way to begin a conversation is to say that you have just executed or updated paperwork related to end-of-life issues and you want the family to understand what you have done, where the papers can be found, and whom they should contact for assistance.

Have the paperwork on hand. Talk about what you did and why you did it and what you expect of your family.

While the paperwork is important, what matters more are the values and hopes we wish to share with the people who care about us and about whom we care. End-of-life conversations are a chance to say the things we think we would regret never saying and the things our family would regret never hearing...and saying them while we are healthy and have time to go forward.

Check out the recommendations on The Conversation Project website.

15. What Happens After We Die?

This question can be understood in its very practical physical interpretation: what happens to my body when I die? Or we can understand the question to be a metaphysical one: what is there for us after our earthly body no longer functions?

I would like to speak to the second question, but I cannot. I have no experience or grounded knowledge and must leave this conversation to clergy and philosophers and those who believe they do have experience. If this interests you, I suggest two people who come to their subject highly schooled in brain function. Jill Bolte Taylor was teaching neuroanatomy at Harvard when she experienced a severe hemorrhage in the left hemisphere of her brain. Her TED talk[26] about realizing her brain is shutting down and her awareness of what is beyond is compelling video(http://www.ted.com/talks/jill_bolte taylor_s_powerful_ stroke_of_insight.html). Her book, *Stroke of Insight,* elaborates on her experience.

The second person, Dr. Eben Alexander III, is a well-trained neurosurgeon who dismissed near-death revelations of God and heaven as explainable by the hard wiring of the brain. However, in 2008, he contracted bacterial meningitis. For a week, his life seemed to be slipping away. His experiences as he faced death changed his views. Risking the skepticism of his medical colleagues, he has written *Proof of Heaven* (http://www.lifebeyonddeath. net/) to describe revelations of God he is sure cannot be explained by brain function.

A different discussion of after-death awareness can be found in *Erasing Death,* Dr. Sam Parnia's book mentioned earlier in the discussion of CPR.

I know many of us focus much more closely on what will happen to our souls than to our bodies, which we know are impermanent. But for a practical moment, can we give some attention to the human body?

"Why should I care what happens after I die?" Fred growls. "I'll be dead and it won't matter to me." Maybe. But after we die, something has to be done with the body. It is conceivable our family will feel they can't afford to deal with our body at all and refuse to claim it or wrap us in plastic and dig a hole in the backyard (illegal in some states but not all.) Or perhaps we or they will decide to donate our body to medical science. But more typically, we assume our families will provide some kind of closure to our time in this world. Have you given them a clue about how to handle this? Our silence is an invitation to disharmony.

Suppose one offspring, wrapped in grief, wants a traditional church funeral with an elegant casket, a trio of limousines for family members, and a reception or wake following. Another offspring, just as saddened, says, "Why would we do that? I'm sure dad would want us to cremate him, bring his ashes to the house, and scatter then in his rose beds with a keg of cold beer." Maybe a third child says, "Look, let's be ecologically sound about this, buy a casket that will return to nature, and we'll bury him in that new green cemetery, even if it is a little far away." And we, alas, are not there to arbitrate while these children have a hell of a fight over, literally, our dead body. If you hate having your family fight, then maybe you do care what happens.

When someone we care about dies, there is grief and, in the middle of this grief are decisions that must be made quickly. Where? When? How? Burial or cremation? Embalming or not? What kind of casket or urn? What kind of service? Have a memorial service or not? Music? Flowers? Food?

Help your family out. Even if you truly don't care, it is likely that the people you leave behind want to do things the way they imagine you would want. So give them some hints. Don't make them fight it out. If you value having an elegant and expensive casket, leave money for it with directions for your service. If you think it's a waste, put it in a letter. If you want to be cremated, write it down. A young chaplain at a local hospital here has planned his entire funeral—music, scriptures, flowers. "I care," he says. "I have opinions based on having been to dozens of funerals, and I have written out just what I would like." One father has told his sons, "Do whatever will make you most happy but if you can't agree, cremate me and be thrifty with your decisions. I would rather you spent the money all going out for a fabulous family dinner where you can toast me."

Making an Exit is Sarah Murphy's fascinating tour of how people in different cultures express grief and hope through their particular burial rituals.:

> For Zoroastrians and Parsis, leaving the dead to the birds reflected their respect for the earth, which they believe should not be polluted with human corpses. Tibetans, on the other hand, see their sky burials—in which corpses are cut into pieces and left as carrion for mountain birds—as acts of generosity to the natural world, with the dead bringing sustenance to living creatures. A similar idea shaped an ancient practice in the Solomon Islands, where corpses were left out on rocks as gifts for sharks.[27]

This should release us from any rigid rules about funerals. There are conventional, accepted ways of mourning a loved one, but there are not, I think, right ways. It is both comforting and helpful to have an established set of rituals to follow when someone we love dies. Most of us need to express sadness and respect, grief and love, and figuring out how best to do that in a stressful moment can feel impossible. Following time-tested patterns and familiar behaviors brings relief and comfort. Unless it doesn't. If you and your family are uncomfortable with what others regard as appropriate, then do what you consider fitting and what will help you celebrate life and give meaning to death.

But here is the challenge. Sometimes those who are living have different ideas about what is appropriate than does the person who died. "Dad loved that blasted church, but I think it's really all a bunch of superstition, and I'm not having a service there," asserts the child responsible for funeral arrangements. So who is the funeral for—the person who died or those left behind? If it is to honor dad, of course, there is a service in that "blasted church." If we are focused on our comfort, perhaps we do things differently. Tell your spouse, your children, your friends, your executor what you want, and if you don't care, tell them what you prefer if no one objects. In this case, maybe there is a church service followed by a memorial a week later in the botanical gardens or the backyard.

Funerals are expensive. The National Funeral Directors Association provides these figures on their website:

Item	Price*
Non-declinable basic services fee	$1,817
Removal/transfer of remains to funeral home	$250
Embalming	$628
Other preparation of the body	$200
Use of facilities/staff for viewing	$395
Use of facilities/staff for funeral ceremony	$450
Use of a hearse	$275
Use of a service car/van	$125
Basic memorial printed package	$125
Subtotal without Casket:	*$4,265*
Metal Casket	$2,295
AVERAGE COST OF A FUNERAL	**$6,560**
Vault	*$1,195*
Total Cost of a Funeral with Vault	*$7,755*

To this, add the cost of the burial plot, on average around one thousand dollars, and the cost of digging the grave, figure another thousand dollars. Still to be considered is the cost of the headstone or grave marker.

Cremation is less expensive. On average, the cost is between two and four thousand dollars if done through a funeral home. It is less if you deal directly with a crematory. Barbara Repa, a senior editor at the website Caring.com, reminds us that there are charges other than burning the body that may or may not be included in the fee:

- Getting an original death certificate and copies.
- Obtaining a certificate releasing the body for cremation, usually issued by a medical examiner or coroner.
- Transporting the body from the place of death to the place of cremation.
- Disposing of the cremains by burying or scattering them.
- Removing a pacemaker.
- Handling charges paid to funeral industry personnel (if involved).
- Purchasing or renting a casket (for a showing) or container.

If you are willing to learn a bit about funerals now, you may save money and aggravation later. I think the quickest and easiest way is to visit the website of the Funeral Consumers Alliance (www.funerals.org/frequently-asked-questions). They have a compendium of questions and answers that explain everything from embalming to organ donation.

A quick read through this section and you will be much better prepared to give directions for your own body and make decisions, if you need to, for someone else's.

There is one other topic connected to what happens to our body. Often, what happens after we die is that those for whom we cared and who care for us grieve. There is no right way to grieve, not even a "normal" way. Some of us weep, and some of us clean house or paint the boat. Some of us feel a great sense of loss that puts a shadow over us for some time. Others regret the loss but accept it and are able to move forward.

If I thought no one would grieve my death, I would have a huge sense of failure. We want people to miss us, to regret that we are no longer laughing and loving with them. But I have told my husband of more than four decades, "Look, I know it will be awful if I die and leave you, but it's bad enough I am dead; you should not feel dead as well. I hope you will go on and live for both of us."

I have always liked the thought that tears are the price we pay for loving; grief is one of many ways we express love.

The experience of grief challenges our deepest sense of who we are. Without help and wisdom we can find ourselves severely and chronically disrupted by the reactions of fear, anger, and isolation arising from grief. Our sense of connection with life itself can seem to disappear.

Yet though overwhelmed by the great upset of grief, we have a choice about how to respond. We can turn away from our own deep pain, seeking relief from distraction, numbing and denial. Or we can turn toward the pain with compassionate attention and a willingness to allow what we are feeling to be just as it is.[28]

There is no formula…do this and say that and this is what will result. But those who work in the field of grief offer some thoughts about what helps.

- Accepting that death is part of life over which we have no control helps to reduce the long-term shock of death. Talking about death and understanding that death happens to all of us in advance of death is one antidote to uncontrollable grief.
- Even if our families are hesitant to acknowledge that we are dying, we can help them by letting them know that we understand what is happening and that we are sad, so let's use the time left for honest and, if possible, joyful communication.
- The ability of a family to be in harmony around difficult decisions can reduce the stress of dying and the trauma of grief.
- Families who use well-designed hospice services and experience death without trauma seem to experience a more peaceful ending with less anxiety.

In his lovely book on aging and dying, *The Force of Character and the Lasting Life*, James Hillman, in his last pages, takes us beyond worry about our bodies in a passage from a twentieth century philosopher, Miguel de Unamuno (1864–1936):

For in fact each man is unique and irreplaceable; there cannot be any other I; each one of us—our soul, that is, not our life—is worth the whole Universe…And to act in such a way as to make our annihilation an injustice, in such a way as to make our brothers, our sons, and our brothers' sons, and their sons' sons, feel that we ought not to have died, is something within the reach of all of us.

All of us, each one of us, can and ought to give as much of himself as he possibly can give—nay, to give more than he can, to exceed himself, to go beyond himself, to make himself irreplaceable.[29]

16. When Is Hospice A Good Idea?

Mary Catherine Bateson calls "Second Adulthood" that time, after our mainstream years, when our responsibilities lessen, our needs are not so insistent, and we are more able to please ourselves.[30] This can be a rewarding time and for some of us, it takes us right through to the end. But some of us, if we don't die along the way, are marched directly into the winds of old age with experiences we do not want. Others are tossed there long before old age. Will pain be waiting? Physical pain? Emotional pain?

It is possible, but fortunately, there are more and better ways to alleviate physical pain than in earlier decades and, often, emotional pain. The miracles of modern medicine have served us in extraordinary ways, but they have also deluded us. We act as if doctors are not only scientists but magicians. If one doesn't have enough magical power, we will find a more potent magician. We will beseech him or her to brew more potions, cast a spell and send the demon of death back to his lair. And damned if sometimes it doesn't work. But neither doctors nor magicians are infallible. A witch's brew can turn you into a horse's ass instead of a prince.

I wish for all of us there were an incantation I could put right here that would send off a white flare if death could be deterred but streak the sky red if medicine had run its course. Instead, we are left to rely on our doctors and our judgment. What I want to say is, please, don't ignore the best medical advice you can get and your own good instincts, but do not imagine that medicine and hope can always trump destiny. Sometimes, the kindest, most helpful thing we can do is open ourselves up to leaving this world and hope to do so with as much grace and peace as possible. Death is not our enemy. It is part of ourselves. We have always been collaborating with death. We have no choice.

I have mentioned Sherwin Nuland's book, *How We Die. Reflections on Life's Final Chapters.* Before explaining, chapter by chapter, the trajectory of the most common diseases, Nuland notes in his introduction:

I have written this book to demythologize the process of dying. My intention is not to depict a horror-filled sequence of painful and disgusting degradation, but to present it in its biological and clinical reality, as seen by those who are witness to it and felt by those who experience it. Only by a frank discussion of the very details of dying can we best deal with those aspects that frighten us the most. It is by knowing the truth and being prepared for it that we rid ourselves of that fear of the terra incognita of death that leads to self-deception and disillusions.[31]

If you read Nuland's book, and I encourage you to do so, you will know that eighty-five percent of aging men and women die from one of only seven diseases, but that is not the important point. What is important is that while many of us die of several of these and some of us from all seven, it is often not the specific disease but the season of our lives that brings death. "The very old do not succumb to disease—they implode their way into eternity."[32] We run down, wear out, cease to be able to resist, and, with or without disease, the curtain comes rumbling down. Hospice can be a good stage setting for one's most final act.

If it is possible to get your mind around this idea, then before sliding into a terminal decline, it is helpful to think about how we want our lives to end. A friend was diagnosed several years ago with pancreatic cancer. Surgery and chemotherapy gave him an unexpected two good years before the cancer roared back. He signed up for more chemotherapy. It made him weak and sick. Finally, his doctors told him he had stopped getting benefit from the treatment, and he was done. They suggested hospice. He wasn't ready to be done. He found doctors who were willing to keep trying and drugs that might work. The treatments made him viciously sick. He was unable to eat or sleep. But he was alive. As I write this, a year later, he is still alive but knows it is only a few months now before he will die. For him, his was the "right" decision. He had another year with his wife and children, more time to spend with his grandchildren. Others of us would not have wanted the year he was given, a year in which he was here but many markers of a good life were gone.

While my friend was enduring his struggle, I received a note about a woman I had worked with in a small training program in public affairs, but we lost track of one another. I so liked this intelligent, energetic woman and was pleased to find a letter in my mailbox with her last name. The note, which came from her son, told me that a few months earlier, she had been diagnosed with ALS, decided against any treatment and had just died in her home with her family at her side. She was still able to speak her goodbyes. She chose to bypass years of treatment and inevitable decline, years in which there still would have been pleasures as well as pains.

There is no right answer. There is no good answer. Each of us tacks our own course, and what we think we want in theory may turn out to be not at all what we want in the face of death. The hunger for life is strong. The challenge is to decide how we define life. These are such difficult decisions, and I don't want to argue that we can pretend they can be made in the abstract. I do believe that we can gear up to make them with more clarity and sanguinity in real time if we think about them in advance.

The happy creation of the hospice movement is one way we can buffer those ill winds. Hospice is where we go to die with good care and comfort. Entering a hospice program requires a physician to certify we have no more than six months to live, but it does not mean we will die within six months. The research tells us that people who enter hospice programs and willingly give up rescue treatment live longer and with less anguish than those with the same conditions who insist that everything medically available be done. It may be that knowing we do not need to fear a painful end and have a support team for us and our families helps the body persevere. In a short YouTube video, a Stanford University Hospital nurse talks about not listening, at first, to her mother and wanting to insist on treatment before a palliative care consult, intended to help patients manage pain and understand their situation, helped this daughter see what her mother really wanted (http://www.youtube.com/watch?v=al2h_1cBnWw).

Hospice and palliative care programs are now widely available, and they are expressly designed to help us control pain and suffering. We do not need to wait until we think we are in our final days to make use of these programs. For the moment, Medicare or insurance coverage of hospice requires a physician to certify that the patient has six months or less to live. We can certainly remain in hospice care longer than six months, but not if we are getting better or even staying stable. Hospice is for people actively dying who agree to terminate rescue treatment (i.e., treatment designed to make them "get better") and instead agree to intensive comfort care intended to make them and their families comfortable and the hospice patients able to die with as little suffering as possible. Many healthcare policy people hope that the hospice requirements will be softened in time so that those with terminal conditions but longer life expectancies can choose hospice care. They speculate that this will help people die with less chaos and will help the healthcare system be more economical. For people like me, who fear pain, hospice is a beacon. There can be a tradeoff. Easing pain may also make us less conscious. Even in hospice, we get to decide what we prefer.

According to the 2012 report of the National Hospice and Palliative Care Organization (NHCPO), nearly forty-five percent of Americans are now dying in hospice care, up from about thirty percent a few years ago. However, half of all these patients spend less than twenty days in hospice care when the greatest benefits seem to accrue to those who enter four to six weeks before they die.

Many hospice patients die from their illness or frailty without assistance. However, hospice does, when it is deemed desirable, use "selective terminal sedation." Using morphine and, perhaps, other drugs, hospice patients who have intractable pain or cannot be calmed in other ways may be sedated (put into a kind of coma without nutrition) and so allowed to await a gentle death. Drugs are not given to end life but to deal with the effects of the illness. If these drugs hasten death, this is known as the "double effect," which means that the management of pain is the intended effect and death is the unintended but inevitable effect. Is this a "natural" death or not? I don't know what "natural" means. I know my mother died this way, and we were deeply grateful she had this choice.

Palliative care, which is newer than hospice care and spreading around the country quickly, does not require, as hospice does, that we forego any treatment. Palliative care is about pain management. Any patient in a hospital with a palliative care program can request a palliative consult. Some hospice programs are beginning to offer palliative care to non-Medicare patients outside the hospice setting, but this is not yet widespread.

The idea of hospice scares some people. "We don't want to raise hospice with my mom because she thinks it means everyone is giving up," a client explained. Another said, "Hospice care means her doctors won't help her anymore." In the most limited sense, these people are right. Hospice means giving up on believing death can be routed. It does not mean giving up on providing intense care and comfort. People in hospice or palliative care programs who are in the same circumstances as people not in those programs actually live longer.[33] It means doctors no longer focus primarily on treatment; now we have doctors who focus on quality of life. An hour-long program from West Virginia public broadcasting offers a look at what kind of care hospice provides (http://www.youtube.com/watch?v=8jKUZ8lS9b4).

The very good thing about hospice care is that it is entirely focused on providing comfort and making the time we have left on earth as rewarding as possible. Ill patients can remain at home with the things and people they love. Hospice doctors are well trained in pain management. Their social workers and chaplains are interested in helping family members as well as the person who is dying. The nurses come every week to visit at home and aides may come as often as every day. In general, these people are very good at what they do and they work together as a team.

But hospice's strength can be its weakness. The majority of hospice patients remain at home. This means there must be people at home to care for them. Kathryn Temple writes in "Unintended Consequences," an essay in *Final Acts: Death, Dying and the Choices We Make*, about her husband's painful death. As he was dying of cancer, the hospital social worker insisted he needed to be enrolled in a hospice program and moved home. Her husband had intractable pain, unpredictable bleeding, and an active case of hepatitis B for which immunization of caregivers requires ninety days. Temple lived in a New York City apartment with a young daughter she wanted to protect from the worst images of her father's illness, was working full time to support her family, and could not afford the full time care she was told her husband needed. He was too young for Medicare and, in any event, the hospital social worker insisted that neither Medicare nor the man's private insurance would pay for in-patient hospice care, which many hospices do not have. Nor would they pay for home care. In theory, hospice offers a "good death," but, in this case, taking her husband home hardly seemed to offer anything good.[34]

Even in less drastic circumstances, caring for a dying person at home presents challenges. Someone must be able to lift the patient if needed, learn to administer meds, and provide basic care. Imagine an eighty-nine-year-old wife with no family nearby doing this for her ninety-year-old husband. Imagine a husband with young children working the night shift and figuring out how to care for his bedridden wife.

Hospice provides a wonderful resource and has a philosophy about accepting dying and preserving quality of life that comforted me when my mother was dying and comforts me when I think of my own death. But it does not take all burdens from the family. It is insufficient when a family cannot manage those burdens. Two of my early readers wrote here, "So tell us what to do." Without money to buy help or a network of family or friends who can help, there are not yet good answers to that question. One possibility is to find an inpatient hospice program if death appears imminent, but this is not always possible. I wish I had better answers. We need those answers.

17. How Do We Talk To Our Doctors?

We respect doctors for knowing things we do not. They understand how the body works and the effects of various medicines and treatments in ways most of us can barely comprehend. They are rigorously trained to rescue us from harm, and we certainly want to be rescued. We deeply admire good doctors for their learning, their commitment, and their passion. But they, like us, are humans. They have strengths and weaknesses. A weakness of many is a disinclination to discuss death and a wish to persist in treatment even if it takes us to a bitter end.

In her compassionate book, *Final Exam*, transplant surgeon Pauline Chen explains how the emphasis on saving patients makes doctors feel like they have failed when the patient is dying. "Along the way, then, we learn not only to avoid but also to define death as the result of errors, imperfect technique, and poor judgment. Death is no longer a natural event but a ritual gone awry."[35] That makes doctors want to turn away from patients who are dying, Chen explains, because they feel they have failed, because they, too, fear death, because they are uncomfortable and don't know how to offer comfort.

It may be their job to recommend treatment, but it is our job to help them be able to talk with us honestly and help us decide if we want these treatments. An article in *HealthDay* spoke of a study in which doctors "…believed that 71% of breast cancer patients rated keeping their breast as a top priority. The actual number was just 7%…" Another study found that patients with dementia placed much less value than doctors on staying alive with severely declining mental functions. And a third study found that patients may change their treatment preferences when informed of the risks and benefits."[36]

The first step in talking frankly with our doctor is talking frankly with ourselves. Our doctors know more medicine than we do. But they can't know us as well as we do. Unless we tell them, they can't know what we value and how we make decisions. So we had better figure out what we value. If, which is the whole point of this book, we can accept that death happens, we are already in a better place to think about what we want and how we need to communicate with our doctors. Then we need to let them know how much information we want and what kind of information.

Take a look at the website of the Informed Medical Decisions Foundation (http://informedmedicaldecisions. org/patient). In addition to information on various health problems, you will find here a good video about the relationship we want with our doctors (http://www. healthdialog.com/Main/Videos/Getting-The-Healthcare-Thats-Right-for-You).

This video will, I hope, reassure you that:

- It is entirely appropriate to get a second opinion.
- It is our responsibility to bring questions and opinions to a meeting with our doctor.
- If our doctor has no time for a reasonable number of questions and for our wish to understand procedures, we should consider finding a new doctor.
- Our doctor should be making decisions together with us. Patient apathy does not help patient or doctor.

There is a kind of comfort in telling our doctor to do what he or she would do or would want for a parent. But we are not all the same: our faith systems differ, our pain tolerance varies, our circumstances are widely diverse. And there is no right answer.

Here are some ways to approach a visit with the doctor:

- Write down your questions and decide which ones are critical. Tell your doctor upfront what you want to be sure to cover.
- Be honest with your doctor. If you are not honest, you cannot expect honesty in return.
- Bring a tape recorder so you can replay the conversation later and/or write down what you are told.
- If you expect there may be complicated or difficult news, bring someone to listen with you and help you remember what occurred. If your spouse is coming, you may still want to bring another pair of ears.
- Ask where you should call if you find you don't understand your instructions.

- Ask where to call if you encounter an emergency when the doctor's office is closed or it is the middle of the night.
- Ask how the doctor wants you handle additional questions.
- Be respectful and acknowledge the pressures your doctor faces. Express thanks at the end of the visit.
- Be prepared to seek another doctor if the one you are seeing makes you feel foolish or if you feel you have been treated with a lack of respect.

I know a woman dealing just now with kidney cancer who told her doctor, "Only tell me what I absolutely must know. Otherwise, tell my husband. I want to know as little as possible about my illness. Denial is a good strategy for me, and I hope you will help me get through my illness this way." I, on the other hand, have told my doctor, "If there is ever anything seriously wrong, I need to be the one you tell first, and I want to know all there is to know as honestly as you can tell it." I have asked him not to talk with my husband, who is both his colleague and friend, without my permission. I know I may need time to think on my own before talking with even the person I love the most.

Some of us want to spend hours on the Internet researching and to ask a zillion questions. Others of us prefer to be told what course of action to follow and then just do it. It used to be harder to opt for the first. Now, with some doctors, it is harder to opt for the latter.

We can't know what to do unless we have sufficient information. That means learning how to listen and how to probe. Not easy in the face of pain, loss, and even death.

For example, our cancer is still marching forward in spite of chemotherapy and radiation. We don't want to die, and our physician doesn't want us to die. Our doctor recommends an experimental treatment which has "a fifty percent chance of prolonging your life." Sounds good, doesn't it? But we have to know first, how long it is likely to extend our time; second, what effects is it likely to have on us; and third, fifty percent of what number. If our chances of survival beyond six months are two percent and we increase those odds fifty percent, we still only have a three percent chance. If the additional time is only a month or two, we need to know that. And if it appears we will spend that extra time seriously ill, we need to know that as well. Most people don't want to worry about the cost of additional treatment, but it is also a factor in these decisions.

We hear what we want to hear. Our doctor tells us a surgery can cure our disease. We imagine we will have the surgery and return to our former state, which is not the same as stopping our disease. We may be told, "There can be consequences from the surgery," but we don't ask what they are, what percentage of patients experience them, and what the alternatives to surgery are. We are optimists and believe optimism is a good strategy. Optimism *is* a good strategy, but ignorance is not. One way to make sure we understand the facts of our illness is to tell our doctor we want to repeat to him or her what we understand about it and be corrected where we are wrong or blind.

In the PLOS blogs, Jessica Wapner summarizes information from a study called the CanCORStudy. Researchers spoke with one thousand one hundred and ninety participants who had stage IV—metastatic, terminal—disease to determine how well patients in chemotherapy understood their condition. "Overall, 69% of patients with lung cancer and 81% of those with colorectal cancer gave answers that were not consistent with understanding that chemotherapy was very unlikely to cure their cancer." More than twenty percent of the patients with lung cancer and more than thirty percent of the patients with colorectal cancer thought chemotherapy was "very likely" to cure their cancer. Almost the same number thought it was "likely." Blame does not always belong to doctors. The researchers found that about one third of patients do not admit that treatment will not cure them.[37]

Do they need to know? Isn't it better to keep hoping until the last breath? Once again, there isn't a right answer. Treatment can give us more time. It can also diminish the quality of the time we have left. It can lead us to avoid the end-of-life conversations that bring closure for us and for those we love. It can also waste money that could better be spent on other healthcare needs. I do not want to debate about who is entitled to what care. We should each decide for ourselves, but we should decide with real information, not fantasy.

The one third that had a discussion with their doctors about their goals for the end were less likely to be in an intensive care unit, less likely to die on a ventilator or be shocked with CPR, and more likely to choose hospice. And the fascinating thing is they suffered less and were more capable and more alert for longer in their lives. Six months after they died, their family members were less likely to be suffering from major depression. Doctors should not hasten death, but we can ask them not to stand in its way when death has come to call for us.

If none of this is easy, it may be comforting to know that it isn't easier for those who live in the medical world. If we feel overwhelmed, confused, ambivalent about what to do, well, so do the experts. Seven medical ethicists, all of whom had cancer and/or had partners with cancer and who worked in medical settings, sometimes the same settings in which they were being treated, wrote an important book about their experiences. In *Malignant, Medical Ethicists Confront Cancer*, Rebecca Dresser says:

> My cancer experience taught me how poorly prepared I was for making important medical decisions. Before I got cancer, I had been teaching and writing about patient autonomy, informed consent, and treatment decision-making for more than two decades. This background was useful, but not as useful as I would have expected…I never thought I might become one of those irrational patients.
>
> Making my own treatment choices was difficult and draining, and…some of my choices were not good ones. Doctors writing about personal experiences with serious illness describe becoming confused and vulnerable when they too become patients…[38]

If those who are most knowledgeable about cancer can feel confused and vulnerable, it makes sense that the rest of us are likely to feel the same way. What helps, these academics report, is having support from others, knowing that resilience is about the capacity to be both vulnerable and strong and being in the presence of love. They learned that without knowing firsthand what it is like to be overwhelmed by the experience of illness, even the most sophisticated clinician may be operating with incomplete information.

What I want for myself is to remember that even the busiest doctor owes me courtesy and compassion. If I can't ask for it myself, I hope those who are speaking for me will make it an expectation. I think it does not help our cause when poor behavior from healthcare providers provokes rudeness or anger from us, even when merited, but I don't think we should just let it go. Better to note aloud what feels callous, rude, or inconsiderate in the kindest but clearest way we can. When our life is in the hands of another, it is hard to challenge that person, but it is harder to be hopeful when we are treated without respect.

18. Can Death Be Funny?

O h yes, of course death can be funny. Maybe that isn't quite right. It isn't that death is funny but that we can be funny about death. Perhaps, you know the term "gallows humor," which is defined in Wiki as "… witticism in the face of—and in response to—a hopeless situation. It arises from stressful, traumatic, or life-threatening situations, often in circumstances such that death is perceived as impending and unavoidable."

Anything as serious and unnerving as dying will bend towards humor as an escape valve. There is reason to believe that laughter counteracts the toll of stress on the body and the immune system, so the more acute our physical situation, the more humor offers some relief. It is not weird or inappropriate to joke in the face of disaster, but it is best that the joking come from those who are suffering and never at their expense.

Death and dying jokes are like ethnic jokes. We joke about our own religion or national origin, but we resent the jokes of those not in our club. I can joke about aging with friends, but I don't like it when my sons joke. The television series *M*A*S*H*, set in an army surgical unit during the Korean War, was a comedy that dealt with the seriousness of war, disaster, and death. That it was one of the most popular television programs ever underscores our acceptance of humor in the face of disaster.

Emergency medical technicians know that humor is a way to dissipate the incredible tensions their work brings. Victoria Corium, a flight paramedic for the Dartmouth-Hitchcock Advanced Response Team (DHART), which supplies ground and air medical transport services all over New England, wrote in an article in the medical school's alumni magazine, "The biggest coping mechanism that we have is dark humor."[39]

But it isn't just medical people who laugh in the face of death. Family and patients see the same release.

A bittersweet example came from an acquaintance whose daughter had leukemia. The daughter's only chance for survival was to have a bone marrow transplant, a difficult and debilitating procedure that requires weeks of isolation. This young woman, in her thirties, endured and, in time returned to work only to find that the transplant was not successful, her cancer had returned, and there was no further treatment. She gave up her apartment in New York City and came home to her parents' house in Houston to die. Her unraveling took several months with increasing decline. One morning, she struggled to come down to the kitchen, looked at her mother, and said, "Dying is such hard work...but I guess someone has to do it."

At his public execution, the murderer William Palmer is said to have looked at the trapdoor on the gallows and asked the hangman, "Are you sure it's safe?"[40]

In his last book, *Mortality*, Christopher Hitchens applies his famous mordant wit to his own condition of terminal esophageal cancer. He observes that he does not understand why people are commonly observed to be "battling cancer" since it seems from his perspective that the cancer is battling him and writes, "in whatever kind of 'race' life may be, I have very abruptly become a finalist."[41]

My mother spent twelve days as a hospice inpatient, dying. She was on morphine to manage acute pain and no longer receiving nutrition or hydration. The days were long and halfway through, I wandered out to the nurse's station and asked the very experienced nurse behind the desk, "Am I nuts? What I'm doing here is killing my mother." She looked at me with great kindness and said, "What are you going to do? Send her to physical therapy?" For me, it was a perfect response. I started to laugh at the ridiculousness of my completely infirm mother engaging in any such activity and, more profoundly, at my complete helplessness in finding ways to "fix" my mother. The laughter was a huge tension release. I immediately felt better, my perspective returned, and I was able to eat a sandwich the nurse ordered from the kitchen for me.

As that difficult waiting period in hospice began, my brother in California agonized over what to do about a trip to China he was scheduled to take in twenty-four hours. "Go, David. This isn't going to end before you are back, and if it does, you have no unfinished business. Mom is not conscious and there isn't anything you can do here." He did go, and my sons, who lived in other cities, called daily to check in on me. My younger son, who was especially close to his grandmother, worried that he should come. I knew it would be very painful for him to see his grandmother dying. He would not handle the situation easily. He had been to visit a few months earlier and already had a sense of closure.

"Don't come," I told him. "Your Nana knew how much you loved her. Stay with your children. When I'm in bed dying, then you can come." There was a long pause before he said, "Nope, if you are going to die like that, I'm going to China."

"Okay," I agreed, "you'll send a Care Bear instead."

Were we callous? Hardly. We were deeply sad, completely loving, and so glad for a bit of lightness. I know Seth is not going to China when I'm dying. But maybe he will wish he could.

A friend's aunt, who was rather vain about her appearance, was in the last stages of dying. She was in morphine-induced coma, and my friend decided it would be a kindness to remove her aunt's false teeth. Coma or no, her aunt bit down on her fingers and would not let those teeth go.

Acquaintances were getting ready to bury their father who had tried to stop smoking many times. He'd manage for a while and then lose the discipline and sneak out to buy a pack. All three of his children, with no coordination, showed up at the funeral home with cartons of cigarettes to be slipped inside the coffin.

My cousin's mother had a bad habit of stealing ashtrays from upscale hotels. Her daughters collected numerous hotel ashtrays from the house and placed them around the funeral parlor. They suggested guests find one and take it home.

It is disrespectful to make jokes about other people's misfortune, but it is, I think, just fine to make jokes about our own. We do want to cry in the face of grief, but there is no need to feel any embarrassment in laughing as well. Not only are we releasing tension; it seems that laughter alleviates pain, boosts the immune system, and improves blood flow to the heart. Dying may not be a joking matter, but I would not mind dying to the sound of loving laughter.

19. Can We End Our Life?

Can we? Certainly, we can. Should we? Will we? Why would we consider this? Would it be an act of courage or cowardice?

Such difficult questions. Our answers are informed by our temperament, our faith beliefs, our fears and hopes, and, just as importantly, our experiences. One of the most compelling arguments heard for giving terminally ill people the right to end life came from the wife of a man who, unresponsive to pain management, died a slow and agonizing death, a dying she watched with her own agony. "We are not supposed to condone torture. My husband was tortured unto death."

And some of the most compelling arguments against assisted suicide come from people like Ira Byock, a much respected hospice doctor who is dedicated to providing pain relief and comfort to the dying. "To fully and authentically affirm life, we must affirm *all of life*, including dying, death, and grief," writes Byock in his book, *The Best Care Possible.* For Byock, human life is "inherently spiritual," and he often finds, in the presence of death, the sacred. He hopes we can create ways of helping people to die with a sense of "inherent meaning despite individual insignificance."[42]

Before we talk about what we think could or should happen, let's look at what does happen. More than eight million Americans appear to seriously consider suicide every year. Thirty-two thousand succeed.[43] Many of these people are physically healthy but suffering from some form of depression. I want to focus our discussion here on men and women over age sixty-five or those younger but suffering from a chronic condition that causes continued suffering. I have not written "fatal" condition since there are some conditions that don't kill us quickly but make our lives seem mean, small, and hopeless.

Men and women sixty-five and older make up about twelve and a half percent of the population. They account for almost sixteen percent of all suicides. This group attempts suicide less often than other age groups but has a greater success rate. It would seem they are not using suicide as a cry for help but as a considered strategy. White men over eighty-five are at a greater risk for ending their lives than people of all other ages, genders, and races. Just under eighty-five percent of elderly suicides have been men, over seven times more than women, and the preferred method, used by seven out of ten men, is a firearm.

Physical illness with uncontrolled pain or fear of a prolonged illness is only one cause. The recent death of a loved one, perceived poor health, social isolation or loneliness, and a major change in social roles are the major reasons for suicide in those over sixty-five. Depression plays a more significant role in younger people, but it is certainly an issue for older people and often can be treated if we allow ourselves to consider that we are, in fact, depressed.

Paul Matteson, eighty-nine, was one of those men who killed himself with a gun. Matteson, much admired by his neighbors for his kindness to them and his wife Mary, who suffered from dementia, shocked the community by shooting Mary, who was in a local care home recovering from a hip operation, and then shooting himself.[44] Do we judge Matteson a criminal for killing his wife? Do we find it odd that people judged so gentle by neighbors left this world in violence? Or is the oddness that Paul Matteson must have thought this awful end was his only reasonable choice?

That Matteson and so many other older men kill themselves each year says, unequivocally, yes we can kill ourselves. But not if we are squeamish, which most of us are when it comes to something so drastic as suicide or euthanasia. What those who favor the right to die on their own terms want is a bloodless, efficient method. Hanging oneself up in the garage, putting a gun to the forehead, or terrifying the train engineer by jumping under his oncoming engine all seem ghoulish and unnecessary in a pharmaceutical age.

The most well-known advocate for our having the ability to end our lives in the face of physical suffering is Derek Humphrey, who founded Hemlock Society USA in 1980 and is past president of the World Federation of Right to Die Societies, both of which support the decriminalization of voluntary euthanasia. The Hemlock Society has become the Final Exit Network and Humphrey's book, *Final Exit*, is a manual for what he terms "self deliverance" and is intended for people hopelessly or terminally ill. It focuses on drug overdose and asphyxia. However, even with a careful and compassionate manual in hand, "self deliverance" is not easy. On November 1, 2007, before my mother became ill, I was driving to her apartment for a visit. *This American Life* was on the radio; the episode was about a mother, diagnosed with Alzheimer's disease, who asked her son to help her orchestrate the end of her life. I sat in my mother's parking lot listening to the story, tears on my face. For me, it was a story of love, courage, and heartbreak. You can listen, too, on episode 342 of *This American Life*.[45]

Let's look at what happens when a bloodless alternative is legally available to people with terminal illness. Oregon's Death With Dignity Act has been in place for fourteen years. Recently the states of Washington and Montana adopted similar acts. In 2012, Massachusetts voters rejected a similar initiative fifty-one percent to forty-nine percent.

In Oregon, two physicians must certify, fourteen days apart, that a person has six months or less to live. If this person asks, twice, for a life-ending prescription, a doctor may then write it. Since 1997, when Oregon's Death with Dignity Act went into effect, slightly more than nine hundred people have received prescriptions to their end their lives. The Oregon Public Heath Division reports that just about six hundred individuals have taken the dose, while the remainder either decided against using the prescription, or succumbed to their diagnosed illness.[46]

Compassion and Choices (http://www.compassion andchoices.org) is a nonprofit organization that helps terminally ill patients and their families make informed and thoughtful end-of-life decisions to hasten a patient's death. In a National Public Radio (NPR) interview with Terry Gross, Judith Schwarz explained that Compassion and Choices does not help people kill themselves nor assist with physician-assisted suicide. It offers information and support so that people can find some ways to control what they are facing.[47]

Our patients, Schwarz explains, "…are dying. They are on a dying trajectory. The only choice they have is the circumstances of their death and what kind of disability they will be suffering as they approach that time." There are, she notes, worse things than dying.

Schwarz continues:

> …the primary reasons for patients asking their physician for the prescription have remained consistent over all those years. It's not about pain; pain can actually be managed…that's not why people want to hasten their dying. They do [it] because they're not able to do any of the things that they've always enjoyed doing—that give them any kind of pleasure. They can't do those things anymore. And they have a complete loss of autonomy, they're dependent upon other people to care for them, and they feel that they've lost all dignity. You have to understand, Terry, this doesn't matter for everybody, but for those people that it does matter to, it matters profoundly. This is really what we think of…as sort of

existential distress—the meaningless of having just to wait for death to occur.

One of those people is T, who is now a hundred and one years old. She and her husband had no children but led a life of engagement with the community. They had many younger friends and were lively and active. When T's husband died, she resisted loneliness and continued to lead an active life, playing bridge, going to concerts, inviting friends to lunch. But in recent years, her life has become more difficult, less active, more painful. She has lost independence, mobility, energy, and, most seriously, interest. She is not, however, ill and no doctor could say she is likely to die in six months. Two years ago, asserting her scarce independence, T took an overdose of medication with the intention of ending her life. Her caretaker, returning early from an evening with friends, rushed her to the hospital where T's stomach was pumped. The experience was "ghastly," and T, who is now never alone, is afraid to have it repeated. She is quite clear to all who know her: "I am done!" Now she waits for her long and lovely life, no longer at all lovely, to end. It is, for her, an end with no pleasure, but at a hundred and one, her capacity to act independently is gone. T evaded all the ills that can surprise us, sidestepped serious accident or debilitating illness, remained alert and competent past a hundred. Her reward, she notes, is misery. Some may argue that this is a fair price for so much happiness, but for T, that seems deeply mean-spirited thinking.

People in three states (Montana, Washington, and Oregon) who are thought to be within half a year of death can be given the means to terminate their lives. People in all states, also within half a year of dying, can enter hospice programs and seek comfort over cure. But people like T or Paul Matteson's wife or C's father, who has not recognized his children or remembered his name for over five years, do not have access to socially acceptable termination or even to hospice comfort care. They are sentenced to time yet to be served.

The American Medical Association opposes any effort to broaden access to assisted suicide. Their position and that of many individual doctors is that the physician's role is to heal, and it is contrary to that role, that pledge to do no harm, to allow physicians to help people die. Dr. Leon Kass, who was the controversial chairman of the President's Council on Bioethics from 2001 to 2005, writes:

> The deepest ethical principle restraining the physician's power is not the autonomy or freedom of the patient, neither is it his own compassion or good intention. Rather, it is the dignity and mysterious power of human life itself, and therefore, also what the Oath calls the purity and holiness of life and art to which he has sworn devotion.[48]

This quote comes from a website called euthanasia.procon. org. You might want to look at their top ten pros and cons for whether euthanasia, the act of directly injecting medication to cause death rather than providing medication for the patient to take if he or she chooses, should be legal. It is banned everywhere in the United States, but is legal in the Netherlands, Belgium, Switzerland, and Luxembourg and under consideration in France. Dr. Marcia Angell, who served for a year as acting executive editor of the *New England Journal of Medicine*, suggests that positions like that of Dr. Kass privilege the physician over the patient:

It seems to me that, as with opposition based on whether the physician is "active," the argument that physicians should be only "healers" focuses too much on the physician, and not enough on the patient. When healing is no longer possible, when death is imminent and patients find their suffering unbearable, then the physician's role should shift from healing to relieving suffering in accord with the patient's wishes. Still, no physician should have to comply with a request to assist a terminally ill patient to die, just as no patient should be coerced into making such a request. It must be a choice for both patient and physician.[49]

Dr. Byock writes that "…when a physician cannot imagine what else to do for someone who is feeling helpless and hopeless, for whom life has no value—…love is the answer."[50] T is graced with people who love her. She is someone who always earned their love. But she insists on remaining in her home and is now isolated. Those who love her cannot be with her all day or even every day. They call, they remind her how much they love her. She is grateful. She is still *"done."* Or rather, she is fervently wishing to be done.

Many worry that opening us up to the possibility of any kind of legal euthanasia will lead to abuse. Will families pressure ill family members to make a quick end? Will we move from allowing the terminally ill to have life-ending prescriptions to encouraging it for others with chronic conditions or long-term disabilities? Will we begin to see euthanasia as a way to reduce healthcare costs, given the millions of dollars Medicare spends on just the last few months of life? Clearly, we don't want that.

Here is what it seems we do want. In a series of eight citizen forums (comprising a total of four hundred sixty-four participants) in New Hampshire convened by Dr. Byock and his colleagues at the Dartmouth-Hitchcock Medical Center, over eighty percent favored removing Medicare requirements of a six-month-or-less life expectancy as well as the requirement to give up disease treatments in order to receive hospice care. Ninety-three percent favored making residential hospice available when needed, and fully sixty percent thought doing so was very important. Over ninety percent wanted physicians to be required to pass tests in basic pain management and end-of-life care in order to obtain licenses to practice medicine and prescribe medication.[51] If we can receive better care in the face of death, we may feel less driven to drastic acts. An Australian physician, Dr. Peter Saul, has a good twenty-minute TED talk about this (www.ted.com/talks/peter_saul_let_s_talk_about_dying.html).

Byock and others involved in death and dying issues believe we can do an even better job of managing pain and fear and providing emotional as well as physical support that removes the desire for suicide. Tivka Frymer-Kensky, a professor at the University of Chicago Divinity School, suggests that if we can think about death in life and have more open discussion, we may be able to face death with more grace. She wonders if we don't need more social rituals for saying goodbye. Dying, letting go of life, scares us. If we can will ourselves to suicide, might we also will ourselves into accepting what is inevitable? Does our culture's emphasis on independence and self-reliance create a loneliness and loss of self-worth that morphine or other drugs can't address? Would people who want to kill themselves because life has lost all luster find that a willingness to move into living arrangements that provide more socialization and more support also provide a more optimistic desire to stick around a bit longer? Or are these cheery thoughts a smokescreen for indignities we simply do not want?

I think we really have not yet begun to have a helpful public conversation about how to address debilitating illnesses that will not yield to treatment, aging processes that deprive us of a sense of vitality and transcendence, and increases in dementia anticipated to affect one in fourteen people over the age of sixty-five and one in six over the age of eighty. I expect we will find better ways to cope, but I do not think we will banish all darkness. We do not condone people killing themselves or those they love. But we seem to condone allowing them to fall into economic purgatory, to suffer from physical and emotional exhaustion with no opportunities to escape and to move beyond the capacity for transcendence or vitality into a space that is neither life nor death. I stand with Frymer-Kensky in thinking that only when we admit death into our life, our personal life, and our cultural life will we have meaningful conversations about how to cope with death.

20. How Do We Find Grace Under Pressure?

With teenagers, we so often insist they "act their age" when acting their age is just what they are doing; it is our expectations that are out of line. Our expectations for growing old, being ill, and dying may also be out of line with reality.

We think that if we lead a healthy lifestyle and work to be young at heart, we can expect to escape decrepitude. We think we can somehow be immune from personal disaster. We think that when we complain, it's justified and when others complain, it is "kvetching."

And if we think we can ignore all there is to learn about death and dying and then get rapid on the job training, dying with grace will be elusive.

What I want to write—because it is what I would love to believe—is that in the face of decline and death, the world will become clearer, my heart will be purer, and I will impart deep wisdom and gratitude to those around me. What I am actually going to write is that odds are good that, as I decline, the world will become more confused, and I may be angry and fearful and show some of my innate grumpiness. I want death to be "interesting." That's because I like interesting, and I dislike painful. Don't think this wish will work out either.

But here is what I do think I can manage, thanks to writing this book and all the work that has led up to it. I hope I will not be surprised that I am going to die. I will not ask "Why me?" I hope I will be able to resist rage. If I will not have found great overall wisdom, I expect to be a bit wiser about how to assess my odds and figure out when it is time to say "enough" to the medical rescue system. And then I hope I can orchestrate staying out of hospital care. Hospitals are good places for getting well. They are not so good for dying.

I am fairly confident I will be able to talk about dying and help those caring for me and loving me to talk about it as well so that I don't have to go out in a fog of pretense. I will not have to spend energy worrying about my business and personal affairs because I have already taken care of the bureaucratic annoyances. I will not pretend that I am having an intense personal growth experience if I am not, and I will not—absolutely not—work on having a "positive mental attitude" if I don't feel like it. But not being positive doesn't mean being negative. I will do my best just to be.

But what about you? What can you do? You can be sure to have thought about what you want at the end of life well before you arrive at the finish line. Let your family know what is important to you. Then do what has always brought you pleasure. If talking with God is a source of comfort, do that. If prayer has provided solace in the past or just feels right in the moment, pray. If being in nature gives you joy, try to be outside some of the time or have the outside come in to you. Spend money on fresh flowers if it pleases you. If you still have digestion, appetite, and taste buds, eat very good chocolate or drink your favorite scotch. If you are social, tell your family you need people around. And if you are not social, be clear that you require solitude with no or few visitors. Make sure the music you like best is playing and the pillows suit you.

Consider having a spiritual guide to help you as you leave this earth. All hospice programs and hospitals have chaplain staffs eager to assist. Compassion and Choices also provides companions to help the dying. Many religious institutions have special assistance for members who are facing death.

Help the people who want to help you by letting them know what you wish. Do not think it is your job to take care of others. Sometimes, our families want us to continue medical treatment when we are done. Sometimes, it is the reverse. Pay more attention to your needs than theirs. Ignore any rules you have about how to die. Die however you damn please. You are only going to do this once and you may as well have your way. But try not to say hurtful things to people who have to stick around and remember them.

We can, once we are limited in what we can do physically, devote our attentions to looking out for beauty, beauty in the natural world, the design world, and the world of human beings. And we can look for humor, for silliness and irreverence and the quick turn of phrase that delights.

We can ask any question. But even at death's door, we want to try to avoid being rude, demanding, or inconsiderate. It does seem that if we must die, we get to suspend those nice civilities that we may have observed in years past, and sometimes pain and fear make us grouchy. But even when we have excuses for being impatient, ill-tempered, or bullying, it is in our own best interests to try to manage civility. When we give in to rude impulses, it can curb the kindness and understanding of others on whom we depend. In the case of Charles Stephens, kindness was his final gift to his family. Here is what his son, Brett Stephens, wrote about his dad in the *Wall Street Journal*:

> He was not a complainer. To bemoan his illness after a life in which the good breaks outnumbered the bad ones would have seemed to him ungrateful. The worst he ever said to me about his cancer was that it was a "bummer."
>
> Yet there was something else at work. The sicker my father got, the more dependent he became on his family, the less he had to give back. What could he offer except not to sink us into the terror he surely must have felt? So he maintained his usual active and joyful interest in our lives and the lives of his friends and in politics and the movies we watched together. Sticking to the mundane and the lighthearted was his way of being protective with the people he loved. For as long as he could muster his wits, death was not allowed to enter the room.[52]

It seems that the trick to finding grace under pressure is knowing how to diminish the pressure. Don't confuse pressure with pain. We may not have the ability to manage away all pain, but it is the internal pressures about which we are talking, those pressures that come from our expectations, our rules, our desires. It is time to suspend them. Just as the past is now truly over and the future has never been more unknown, we are, in the face of death, most intensely in the present. Every moment is all we have.

Organizing a Death, Dying and Dessert Group

A Death, Dying and Dessert group need not have dessert, although it sweetens everything. Really, all that is required to begin is one or two people who hold firmly the intention to start talking about death and dying. Recruit a few others. We started our group with five members. That number seemed fine. As others heard us talk about the group, they asked to join and that was fine, too. We started with one group around the dining room table. When more women wanted to join than our tables could accommodate, we formed a second group and, in time, we merged the two groups and abandoned the table. We have had as many as twenty-one people join the conversation. Usually, there are between eight and fifteen of us, and that seems to work.

I think what makes this group so successful for us is that nobody brings a point of view she wants to foist on others. We don't all see the world the same way, but there is no judgment of those with different views. Some of us are deeply religious; others are agnostics or atheists. We are Christians and Jews and Buddhists. A Muslim member would be welcome if she appeared. Some of us lead with our hearts and others with our heads, but there is a shared sense of mutual respect. We are married, widowed, single, with and without children, working or not. Our ages range from barely fifty to eighty.

Our group, which grew out of a professional women's group for women over age fifty moving from their mainstream lives to what's next (originally affiliated with The Transition Network [TTN] and now independent and called Women in Transition [WIT]) is all women, but it could be all men, mixed genders, one faith or many faiths. It can meet day or evening and as often as the group wishes. It can meet anywhere, although some place that feels more relaxed than instructional is probably good.

We now meet every six to eight weeks at the same home. People aim to arrive around 6:00 p.m. Everyone chips in ten dollars for a light supper, and we socialize. Around 6:45 p.m., we usually start our serious conversation. Each evening has a specific conversation topic. Susan Lieberman always facilitates the conversations. "But," she says, "I'm not the leader. There is no leader. I'm the glue." Leader or glue, it is helpful to have one person who serves as the coordinator and makes sure topics are chosen, emails are sent, and socializing yields to the conversation at hand.

A group might want to use the chapters in this book as conversation topics or borrow from the topics we have used for Death, Dying and Dessert since we began in 2009:

1. **Imaging Death**

   Assuming I have reason to believe that my death may be near at hand, within weeks or months, how do I imagine I will have arranged my circumstances internally and externally?

2. **Fears**

   When I think about death and dying, what are the things that I fear, the things I don't even want to tell myself inhabit worrisome crinkles in my brain?

3. **What Does Death Look Like**

   Bring a visual representation of what death looks like to you.

4. **Ethical Wills**

   What is the non-material legacy we hope to leave behind and do we want to write it down.

5. **Our Paperwork**

   Are our papers ready for us to die? Do we have the completed forms we ought to have? What are they and where are they and when will we have them complete. (wills, Croak Book, medical directives, etc.)

   We invited an estate attorney to join us for this conversation.

6. **Listening to Older Women**

   We invited four women older than we to talk with us about what they have observed in their own aging and death-approaching years.

7. **Control of Death/Assisted Suicide**

   If we wanted to manage our own death, how might we do it?

   We invited a medical ethicist to join us for this conversation.

8. **Choosing Care**

   What do we see as the choices for our living arrangements and care if needed as we age? What do we think about the choices?

9. **Positive Mental Attitude**

   How do we ward off narcissism, self-centeredness, anger, or other unappealing behaviors when we feel rotten, depressed, afraid....or, more important, can we control not feeling those negative emotions?

10. **Success in Old Age**

    What is our template for success in this post-mainstream stage of development? Will it change yet again?

11. **Stereotypes**

    We know there are stereotypes for older women. Which ones do we unconsciously and incorrectly embrace... and which are true for us?

12. **After We Die**

    What happens to our body? Do we have opinions about funerals, memorials, etc.?

13. **Chaplaincy**

    We invited Hope Lipnick, a chaplain at the Houston Hospice at the Texas Medical Center, to talk with us about end-of-life conversations.

14. **Talking to Our Healthcare Proxy**

    How do we talk to our healthcare proxy and our other family members about our end-of-life issues?

15. **Dialogue With Death**

    Imagine sitting in a chair with death facing you in another chair. What would you want to say to death?

And what do you think death would choose to say back to you?

16. **Aging**

What bothers us about our own aging and is there anything to do about it?

17. **Loss of Independence**

What happens when we refuse to recognize that we need to give up some of our independence? What have our parents' experiences taught us?

18. **Learning to Ask for Help**

Can we begin now thinking about how to ask for help in ways that will be comfortable for us?

19. **Finding Support**

How can we find support when it's needed but family/ friends are not available? (This conversation led to a special meeting with faculty who train geriatric nurse practitioners.)

20. **Mortality**

We agreed that we would read and discuss Christopher Hitchens's book *Mortality*.

21. **Grief**

What have we learned about facing grief?

22. **Faith**

What role can our faith play in helping us face death and grief?

Appendix II

Geriatric Care Managers

H ire a geriatric care manager to help you plot a course of action.

You can do this by going to the national website of the National Association for Professional Geriatric Care Managers www.caremanager.org), all of whom have a professional certification. I live in Houston. I typed my zip code into the website and was given a list of thirteen people within a tenmile radius of my house. Call a few and talk on the phone and decide who sounds right. An alternative is an experienced social worker.

What if you live in an area where there are no certified managers? Just as a test, I typed two small Texas cities into the association's locator, Fort Stockton, Texas (population 8,404) and Brownwood, Texas (population 19,329). No results came up for either zip code, even when I allowed a hundred-mile radius. It is possible you do not live in an area with this service. Consider a geriatric case manager anyway. Find a city where such people exist, or find someone in a city where other members of your family or even good friends live. Use them as consultants on the phone and/or on the Internet. Some may travel for a fee.

You do not need to use these services for an extended period of time. What you want is someone to coach you through understanding what decisions you need to make and what the critical questions are. You may want to use this person as a sounding board as you get started and then circle back for an hour now and then. Typically, hourly rates for these care managers are between fifty and two hundred dollars an hour. Here in Houston, a case manager I know and respect charges one hundred dollars an hour.

The Geriatric Care Manager Association lists the kind of support that care managers often provide:

- Housing—helping families evaluate and select appropriate level of housing or residential options
- Home care services—determining types of services that are right for a client and assisting the family to engage and monitor those services
- Medical management—attending doctor appointments; facilitating communication between doctor, client, and family; and if appropriate, monitoring client's adherence to medical orders and instructions
- Communication—keeping family members and professionals informed as to the well-being and changing needs of the client
- Social activities—providing opportunity for client to engage in social, recreational, or cultural activities that enrich the quality of life
- Legal—referring to or consulting with elder law attorney, providing expert opinion for courts in determining level of care

- Financial—may include reviewing or overseeing bill paying or consulting with accountant or client's power of attorney
- Entitlements—providing information on federal and state entitlements; connecting families to local programs
- Safety and security—monitoring client at home; recommending technologies to add to security or safety; observing changes and potential risks of exploitation or abuse.

There is a good chance you will need help with more than one of these. Read Gross' helpful article in the archives of the *New York Times*' New Old Age Blog, which talks about the role of managers (http://newoldage.blogs.nytimes.com/2008/10/06/why-hire-a-geriatric-care-manager/).

If you are taking care of a parent, don't be afraid to use parental funds to pay for the care manager. You can always use your own funds later, and if you need to spend down a parent's funds to qualify for Medicaid, this will work to your advantage.

Appendix III

Supplemental Letters

Dear Lori and Michael,

I am writing this on a windy winter afternoon, not long before a new year will begin. This is a time when my thoughts turn to the future and events over which I will have no control. As my "days dwindle down to a precious few," I think more often about how my life will end... because, much as you don't like to talk about it, it will. I hope for a peaceful end, I hope you will be beside me, to hold my hand in those final seconds. Of all the things I fear about dying, what I fear most is dying alone.

Like most parents, I dread becoming a burden to my children, so I've given you what I hope you'll agree is a gift. I've put a deposit on an apartment in a Continuing Care Retirement Community. It is an independent living place for active seniors like me, but it has levels of care—assisted living, skilled nursing, facilities for Alzheimer's patients. Once I'm living there, beginning in 2015, you'll know that in a crisis you won't have to search desperately for a place for me. And just think, you won't have to worry that I'll call one day blubbering, "My roof is leaking and I don't know what to do." Not only will I not have a roof, but if something goes wrong in my apartment, I can just call maintenance to fix it. You won't have to become my chauffeurs when I can't drive any more. Transportation is provided. So this is a gift for all of us: peace of mind for you and security for me.

This is not to say that a health crisis won't happen. We've talked about my wishes for the end of life. If I'm beyond help, please don't keep me alive…because I won't be alive, not really. Seek palliative care for me. I don't want to suffer unbearable pain. I have no desire to die at home. I can't imagine how difficult that would be for you to deal with. Hopefully, I'll be able to participate in the choice of places. I've been told hospice allows pet visits. Wouldn't that be comforting? So hospice, hospital, the Continuing Care Community—so long as you are there for my final moments, any of the three would be all right.

Finally, I don't want to wait until the end to tell you how much I love you and how proud I am of both of you. And special thanks to Michael and Monica for giving me the gift of Gabriella.

I'd love to live to be a healthy, alert centenarian, but if not, I'm thankful for the life I've had, and I want you to remember that.

With love,
Mom

Dear Daughters,

I just watched President Obama deliver his second inaugural address. I frankly never expected to live long enough to see an African-American elected two times to this high office. Then again, that is only one of several surprising events that I have witnessed: I've seen men walk on the moon, snow melt off Mount Ararat's peak in less than thirty years, and the Philadelphia Phillies win the World Series twice.

Growing older has been memorable. I am eligible to retire under Social Security in a few weeks. That should hardly seem remarkable—after all, millions of baby boomers are splashing in "Golden Pond." Like most of my peers I have enjoyed successes (professional and personal); I count maintaining longstanding friendships to be my greatest contribution. The ironies and paradoxes of late life do not surprise me, but particular memories and images make me glory in each day. Of course I have had my share of travails: I now bite my tongue because your feud rips me apart. Offering courses on aging for nearly four decades has taught me that it is one thing to teach about students about life and another to experience it. Truth be told, I never expected to be around, much less feeling so fully alive, so happy to hold grandchildren, to plan ahead for death.

Nor is death a stranger to me. I have buried my parents, a brother, and an increasing number of friends and colleagues. I know men and women who live too long, or so they say. I know that frailty and dementia are not fun. Such occurrences are risks to everybody else, including me. Having nearly died three times--at age seven, then at age forty, and most recently at age fifty-six—I am aware that I will die someday. Being sixty sometimes feels like forty, just as AARP trumpets, but I doubt that if I reach ninety that I will feel like I do now. I would like to control the timing and manner of my last months, but there are too many contingencies at stake for me to be assured that I will get my way. Dying is the mystery that scares me.

I have taken steps to prepare for dying. My primary care physician and I have discussed options that I want and do not want. I update my will every other year. We discussed the latest version of that document a few days after Luke was born. Emily, you peppered me with hypothetical situations; Laura, who nursed me so well through cancer, you raised good ethical concerns. This was not the first conversation we have had; it will not be the last.

I vacillate about how to balance my own private wishes and the public expectations of others. I am a religious person, but I know you girls and most of my friends are not. For all of you I would like to think that I will leave a legacy of love and hope, not entirely in conformity with social norms and prescriptions. I definitely want to receive last rites (please ask Barbara to perform this ministration), but today I remain inclined to leave funds for a big cocktail party in lieu of an Episcopal funeral service. I want my body given to science, the ashes shared, and the rest sprinkled over my family's plot near Philadelphia. Let my brother help you with arrangements.

I do not know what follows next. Nor do I much care. I take great comfort in knowing that you two loved me as deeply as I have cherished you. I trust that death will not sever this bond. I look forward to being pleasantly surprised.

Love, Dad

.....

Dear Family,

I write as I approach my seventy-second birthday happy and in good health, and really among the most fortunate of men. I was born and have lived in a window of good fortune and possibility and have been lucky in my marriage, my family, and my work. I do not feel I have important life tasks remaining, which is not to say that I do not enjoy living or feel engaged or eager to embrace life; however, the realization that I have lived a full and happy life, that I have not left things undone decidedly informs these instructions. At this moment I feel completely centered in my life, which makes the consideration of my death an emotionally easy but non-trivial task.

If I should become incapable of making decisions and anything in these instructions and my other end-of-life documents is ambiguous or unclear, my beloved should make decisions in consultation with my sons and their wives, or if she is incapable of doing so, my sons in consultation with their wives.

While I Am Alive
If I have to choose between living a diminished life and dying, I would like to die. By diminished, I mean mentally

unaware by reason of a severe stroke, senility, Alzheimer's disease, or similar incapacitation. I do not want to live as a quadriplegic, a severe hemiplegic, or even a paraplegic. If a have a terminal illness such as endstage cancer or a severe cardiovascular event, let me die. If I develop a severe "no-exit" neurological disease such as Lou Gehrig disease or crippling Parkinsonism, let me die. I do not mean to be macabre about these conditions or cavalier about my life, but there are no compelling lifecycle events (the graduations or marriages of my grandchildren, etc.) that I feel I must be present for. I would rather my family remember me as the vigorous person I am rather than the diminished person I will have become.

If I have one of these conditions or something similar, I urge my family to be as proactive as possible in hastening my death, or if that is not possible, insisting that I be deeply sedated. I do not fear death, but I do fear pain. I would prefer hospice to futile hospital heroics. I only ask that in following my instructions, no family member puts him or herself in harm's way. Do not do anything that would have serious legal consequences for one of you. On the other hand, covert collusion is, in my opinion, an honorable and desirable course of action.

As for prayers and ceremonies prior to my death, I do not feel the need for any. I do not wish to be visited by clergy, except those who are friends. At this moment I am centered in my life. If, however, family members feel the need for a religious or spiritual ceremony or counsel, I have no objection. Let love, good judgment, clear thinking and practicality dictate your actions.

After I Am Dead

All things being equal, I prefer to be cremated in a simple, inexpensive way. However, I have no objection if family members feel it important to buy a plot in a cemetery and bury me (headstone and all). It is superfluous to add that in the event of a burial I prefer a Jewish or a nondenominational cemetery. As for the service, I have no need of a religious service, though I have no objection to a Jewish service or a non-religious spiritual service. As for my ashes, I do not consider the irreducible mineral of my bones ashes. On the other hand I have no objection to my family's scattering these anywhere or in any way that they choose. In all these matters, the needs of my living family should prevail over mine.

Should there be a gathering, I ask that someone read Polonius's speech from *Hamlet* act 1, scene 3 (the one containing "above all to thine own self be true. . .") and other readings and poems as people see fit. I also hope the gathering will be private with family members and a few close friends that the family may choose to invite. I have no need to have my obituary published in any newspaper, but I do not object to the family's doing so if it seems important to them.

I hope my family will remember me fondly but look to the future and move on quickly with their lives, that my wife will develop a close relationship or remarry, that my children will focus on their lives and their children. Grief should have a six-week statute of limitations. Remembrance has no statute of limitations, but neither does it have a veto over the practical needs of the family.

If friends or family desire to make donations to institutions, I ask they be directed to my alma mater and other causes that are consistent with a liberal philosophy (as it has been understood in the late twentieth and early twenty-first century.)

My will and wishes with respect to my grandchildren are known to all of you: that we all do the best we can for this generation. Specifically, however, if special needs emerge among one or more of them—meaning that they have some handicap or exceptional gift that as of now is not apparent—I ask that some of my worth be used to ensure that they prosper. I, of course, mean this to be the need for resources beyond what we usually think of as funds for college, etc.

Last, I have no need to be remembered beyond our family's present generations. The generations pass, the living making their mistakes and their contributions, and so it has been with me. I am not vain enough to believe that anything I have said or done is so unique or special that it warrants any attempt at preservation. As you know, I have written a memoir providing reflections on my life and our married life together. I have set aside a printed copy of the memoir for each of my grandchildren. My hope is that each will receive one, not with the idea that there is some special wisdom here, but rather with the hope that one or two of them may have some curiosity about who their grandparents were as people. As we have all remarked, one unfortunate aspect of our family is the length of the generations, which makes it all but impossible for our grandchildren to know us as people. The memoir may give any who is interested a sense of our thoughts and concerns, our passions as individuals, and both our strengths and our weaknesses.

With great love.

.....

Dear Children:

We are writing this letter to let you know about our wishes regarding our endoflife care. This is being written at a good time in our lives, when both of us are healthy and enjoying life, and able to articulate what the two of us have discussed often with each other, and occasionally with you. Having these general guidelines in written form should give you additional support in the event that one or both of you become responsible for making decisions for us in the future.

Both of us have living wills and medical powers of attorney. Our living wills make clear that we do not want our lives artificially maintained if we are in terminal or irreversible conditions. Sometimes, even with these documents in place, confusion can reign, especially in the case of sudden onset of a serious illness or accident. We hope these general principles will make even clearer what our wishes are.

First, some thoughts about artificial life support. What we mean by this term is any device, procedure, or medication that can be used to keep a person alive. These include ventilators, dialysis, tube feedings of both food and water, cardiopulmonary resuscitation, blood transfusions, antibiotics and pressors (medications designed to raise blood pressure), chemotherapy, and surgery. Often, these can be of great benefit to people. We can imagine that there would be a time when they would be acceptable. But the key for us is whether these procedures would lead to an improved state of health, with mental faculties intact, or would be performed in order to simply delay death. They would be acceptable to us in the former case, but not in the latter. The same is true if we were to be in a comatose state from which we would not be expected to recover, or with severe brain damage that rendered us permanently unable to care for ourselves, be aware of our environment, or recognize loved ones.

In all cases we would want to receive aggressive pain management or, if at the end of life, sedation.

If we are hospitalized, you should work closely with the doctors and other staff to get regular updates on our conditions and prognoses. Don't be reluctant to ask for regular meetings with those knowledgeable about our conditions. Physicians can be reluctant to give family members less than hopeful information involving loved ones. Let the staff know you want honest, straightforward answers to your questions. Ask for second opinions if you are in doubt about limiting or refusing life-sustaining treatment.

Finally, many hospitals offer palliative care and hospice services, where care is redirected strictly toward comfort. We would want you to choose these options for us once the decision is made to stop life-sustaining treatment.

We hope this gives you a good idea about how to proceed in the case that we're unable to make our own healthcare decisions, especially at the end of life. Don't be afraid to make difficult decisions. We trust that your love and judgment will guide you to do what's best.

With love and affection,
Your Parents

.....

Dear Gabriel and Moriah,

My sweet children. If you are reading this, it means my soul has moved on to a better place and you are trying to figure out what to do with my body. First, know that I am fine. I have never been afraid of death and have always believed in everlasting life beyond this physical one. I am sorry to be separated from you because you have been the joy and loves of my life. I promise to watch over you still. (I've always wanted to be an angel!)

I remember how devastating it was for all of us to lose Dad so suddenly in 2008. You were only seventeen and fourteen and it was overwhelming, even for me, to make all the funeral arrangements in such a hurry and under such stress and grief. I want to help make this easier for you by letting you know what I'd like.

First, simple is good. I'd rather you spend money on a great trip than an expensive funeral. Pick out an inexpensive casket and dress me like you remember me; don't forget earrings and a shawl. Those were my trademarks. If possible, I'd like to have a viewing so I could say goodbye to my wonderful friends one last time. And while I know that might be harder for both of you to greet all the well-wishers, I want you to see all the people who will still be around to support you and love you after I'm gone. Don't restrict flowers (they are my favorite thing!), but also encourage donations to be made in my honor to MANA Nutrition. This was the cause of my life. I hope Mark Moore is still around to receive the donation…and in fact, I'd love him to do the funeral if he's up to it. Otherwise, just pick someone you're comfortable with.

If possible, I'd love to have the funeral in a church; First Methodist, where Dad's funeral was, is my preference; but anywhere will do. Music does matter and it would make me happy to have the music include the singing of "Amazing Grace," "It is Well with My Soul" and the "Hallelujah Chorus". Have someone read Psalm 40; it has always been a beacon for me. I'd like to be buried next to Dad, but if that's not possible choose a place that you think I'd like; with trees if possible. A simple marker with my favorite quote by Van Gogh inscribed "I am seeking, I am striving, I am in it with all my heart."

Throughout this letter I have said "if possible." I do this because I am simply trying to make your decisions easier, not make requirements or bind you with "last wishes." My life is over and I am on to a new adventure. I will be happy with any decisions you make. Surprise me if you want.

This, however, is my last dying wish. Be happy; be well; find love and meaning every day.

When you were both very young, our minister Bill Hinson (I know you remember Pastor Bill) was going on a trip to the Holy Land and said that while on the trip he would climb Mount Sinai early one morning, before the sun came up, to pray. He offered to pray a prayer for anyone who would write it on a piece of paper and give it to him before he left. Let me say that I have always been a prayer and always believed in the power of prayer. But I definitely don't believe that anyone's prayers are more powerful that anyone else's, and that goes doubly for clergy. I also don't believe prayers are more powerful if prayed in the Holy Land or the New York subway... or your car. But for some reason, Bill's request sent me on a soul-searching journey I will never forget. It was as if what I put on that paper would be granted and therefore needed to be the reflection of my heart's deepest desire—the one thing I wanted most in life. I went through the usual suspects—health, happiness, security. But after weeks of deep thought, I wrote this on the piece of paper I gave him:

God, please instill in my children, Gabriel and Moriah, a deep and abiding faith that will give them strength, guidance, peace, lovingkindness, and joy no matter what they face in their lives.

This is still my heart's deepest desire. I love you to the moon and back.

Mom

. . . . .

Appendix IV

The Croak Book

A ppendix IV was originally intended to include Jim Steinback's complete Croak Book. On further thought, it seemed more useful for readers to have these pages available in full 81/2 X 11 size and to be able to type information directly onto the pages. Therefore, what is included here are the chapter headings in the Croak Book and a link to the entire PDF on the www.SusanLieberman. com website where it can be downloaded for free.

http://susanlieberman.com/croak-book.pdf

Many of you who read this will find yourselves in less affluent circumstances than the people for whom this was originally prepared and have less detailed estate needs. I am reprinting the Croak Book as Jim Steinback has written it because it can help people with very complicated financial circumstances, but it can easily be adjusted by those of us who have more modest resources. Do not let the details of high income deter you from using this valuable resource.

The Croak Book includes the following sections as Jim Steinback prepared them in 2009. With Jim's permission,

I have added a final section as an addendum at the end for computer password information.

Croak Book Sections

......

Jim Steinback has shared his work without reward. If you find what he has provided of value to you and would like a way to say thank you, consider a donation to the Sonia Shankman Orthogenic School in Chicago, IL. Jim and his wife, Jo, are long-time board members, and Jim spearheaded the capital campaign to build a new building.

Jim describes the school:

> One school is a residential program through high school for kids with serious emotional handicaps. It's been on the campus of the U of C for seventy years. The other is a day program for kids through eighth grade with learning disabilities, started in 2000. A few years ago the University informed the board that they wanted their building back and gave the school five years to depart. That was a down day, but we've since turned lemons into lemonade. One by one, we acquired thirty-five lots less than a mile away, worked with the City, raised the equity, borrowed some money, and are now eleven months away from having a new, twenty-nine million dollar, seventy-three hundred square foot building on over three acres with a green roof, PV solar panels, and

room to add forty more children. When at capacity, the Schools collectively will have two hundred children. These schools are simply the best in the business.

To learn about the Orthogenic School and make a donation go to http://orthogenicschool.uchicago.edu/about.html and click on the DONATE button on the left side of the screen.

Endnotes

1   Morris, Deborah, Talking About Death (Chapel Hill: Algonquin Books of Chapel Hill, 2001) P. 3.
2   Morris, p. 108
3   *New York Times,* A Quest to Understand How Memory Works by Claudia Dryfus, 3/5/12
4   Becker, Ernest, The Denial of Death (New York: Simon and Shuster, Free Press Paperbacks, 1973) p, 66
5   Becker, p. 87
6   Becker, p. 90
7   Becker, p. 190
8   http://www.livescience.com/6274-age-bring-happiness-despair.html
9   Agronin MD, Mark E., *How We Age. A Doctor's Journey Into The Heart Of Growing Old* (Philadelphia: Da Capo Press, 2011) p.12
10 Agronin, p. 65
11 Jacoby, Susan, *Never Say Die. The Myth and Marketing of The New Old Age* (New York: Pantheon Books, 2011) p. 295
12 Agronin, p. 204
13 Jacoby, p. 6
14 From an epigraph in John O Hara's novel. See "Story of Samarra" in Wiki.
15 The best is not smoking.
16 Nuland, Sherwin, *The Art of Aging, A Doctor's Prescription for Well-Being* (New York: Random House, 2007), p. 43-44
17 Nuland, *Aging,* p. 237
18 Hitchens, Christopher, *Mortality* (New York: Twelve, 2012) p. 57
19 Wang, Penelope, "Cutting the high cost of end-of-life care," *CNN Money,* 12/12/12
20 I used Wikipedia for information on these summaries and it provides good reporting on both cases.
21 http://www.compassionandsupport.org/videolibrary/community_conversations_on_compassionate_care_videos.php#

22 This is tool #7 in the American Bar Association's healthcare tool kit:
www.americanbar.org/content/.../aba/.../tool7.authcheckdam.p.

23 Alicia Gallegos, "Clearing up confusion on advance directives," amednews.com, 10/29/12.

24 http://www.thehastingscenter.org/Publications/BriefingBook/Detail.aspx?id=2198

25 "Medical Myths" bu Dr. Robert Shermerling in InteliHealth on the web, 10/23/12.

26 TED (Technology, Entertainment and Design) is a global set of conferences owned by the private non-profit Sapling Foundation, formed to disseminate "ideas worth spreading." Since June 2006, the talks have been offered for free viewing online. As of November 2011, over 1,050 talks are available free online. In June 2011, the viewing figure stood at more than 500 million, and on Tuesday November 13, 2012, TED Talks had been watched one billion times worldwide, reflecting a still growing global audience.

27 Murray, Sarah, *"Making an Exit. From the Magnificent to the Macbre – How We Dignify the Dead* (New York: St Martin's Press, 2011), p. 101

28 Kumar, Sameet. "*Grieving Mindfully* (Oakland: New Harbinger Publications, 2005). From the introduction by Dr. Jeffrey Brantley at the Duke Center for Integrative Medicine, p. viii

29 Hillman, James, *The Force of Character and the Lasting Life* (New York: A Ballantine Book, 1999), p.200

30 Bateson, Mary Catherine, *Composing a Further Life. The Age of Active Wisdom* (New York: Knopf, 2010

31 Nuland, *How We Die,* p. xvii

32 Nuland, *How We Die,* p, 83

33 Connor, Stephen; Pyenson, Bruce; Fitch, Kathryn, Spence, Carol RN, MS, and Iwasaki, Kosuke, "Comparing Hospice and Nonhospice Patient Survival Among Patients Who Die Within a Three-Year Window,"

34 Temple, Kathryn, "Unintended Consequences: Hospice, Hospitals and the Not-So-Good Death, *Final Acts, Death, Dying and the Choices We Make* edited by Nan Bauer-Maglin and Donna Perry (New Brunswick: Rutgers University Press, 2012) pp.183-203

35 Chen, Pauline, *Final Exam* (New York: Vintage Books, 2007), p.95

36 Preidt, Robert, http://consumer.healthday.com/Article.asp?AID=670509, Health Day, 11/8/12

37 Wapner, Jessica, "Why Do People With Advanced Cancer Undergo Chemotherapy?" PLOS Blog, (http://blos.plos.org), 12/10/12.

38 Dresser, Joy, editor, *Malignant. Medical Ethicists Confront Cancer* (New York: Oxford University Press, 2012), p. 64

39 *Dartmouth Medicine,* the Dartmouth Medical School's alumni magazine, 2005.

40 I found this story in a Wiki article on gallows humor.

41 Hitchens, *Mortality,* p. 4

42 Byock, Ira, *The Best Care Possible. A Physician's Quest To Transform Care Through The End Of Life* (New York: Penguin Group, 2012), p. 282 and p. 294.

43 http://www.huffingtonpost.com/2009/09/17/8-million-americans-consi_n_290075.html

44 http://www.mlive.com/news/jackson/index.ssf/2012/07/absolutely_shocked_to_hear_it.html

45 http://www.thisamericanlife.org/radio-archives/episode/342/how-to-rest-in-peace?act=2

46 Joyce, Jaime, "The Evolving State of Physician-Assisted Suicide," *The Atlantic,* 7/16/12, http://www.theatlantic.com/health/archive/2012/07/the-evolving-state-of-physician-assisted-suicide/259862/

47 Find the podcast at http://www-cdn.npr.org/rss/podcast.php?id=13, 10/09/12

48 http://euthanasia.procon.org/view.resource.php?resourceID=000126

49 Angell, Marcia, "May Doctors Help You Die, New York Review of Books, 10/12/12

50 Byock, p. 284

51 Byock, p 276

52 Stephens, Brett, "A Lesson Before Dying," *The Wall Street Journal*, 12/13/11

Additional books can be ordered from
susanlieberman.com or Amazon.com